GALVESTON COOKBOOK FOR BEGINNERS

1800 Days of Fast and Easy Anti-Inflammatory Recipes for Optimal Wellness and Hormone Balance, Complete with a 28-Day Meal Plan

Alise Rosalin

TABLE OF CONTENTS

CHAPTER 5: DINNER — 47

CHAPTER 6: SNACKS AND SIDES TO SATISFY YOUR CRAVINGS — 57

CHAPTER 7: SWEET TREATS FOR GUILT-FREE INDULGENCE   67

CHAPTER 8: BEVERAGES TO HYDRATE AND REFRESH   75

CHAPTER 9: FISH AND SEAFOOD   83

CHAPTER 10: POULTRY AND BEAF RECIPES 91

CHAPTER 11: SALADS RECIPES 99

.

CHAPTER 1: UNDERSTANDING THE GALVESTON DIET

Embarking on the journey of the Galveston Diet unfolds a new chapter in understanding how the food we eat can profoundly impact our health, wellness, and overall quality of life. At its core, this diet is more than just a pathway to weight loss; it's a lifestyle shift toward eating mindfully, with an emphasis on foods that combat inflammation, balance hormones, and nurture our bodies.

The Galveston Diet stands out for its scientific foundation, focusing on anti-inflammatory eating and the crucial role of hormone balance in achieving optimal health. It's designed not only to guide you through shedding those stubborn pounds but also to enhance your energy levels, improve your mood, and elevate your overall well-being.

As we delve into this chapter, we'll explore the pillars of the Galveston Diet, starting with an introduction to anti-inflammatory eating. You'll learn why some foods cause inflammation—a condition linked to a host of chronic diseases—and how choosing the right foods can help mitigate these effects. We'll also discuss the significant impact of hormone balance on weight management and overall health, providing insights into how the Galveston Diet supports hormonal harmony.

The journey to better health through the Galveston Diet is as enlightening as it is transformative. It's about making informed choices that not only bring you closer to your weight goals but also contribute to a vibrant, healthier you. By the end of this chapter, you'll have a solid understanding of the foundational principles of the Galveston Diet and be ready to embrace the changes that lie ahead. Together, let's embark on this journey to wellness, equipped with knowledge and inspired by the promise of a healthier tomorrow.

INTRODUCTION TO THE GALVESTON DIET

Welcome to the beginning of a transformative journey with the Galveston Diet, a path that intertwines the science of nutrition with the art of living well. This diet is not just a temporary fix or a one-size-fits-all solution; it's a lifestyle that embraces the power of anti-inflammatory foods to enhance your health, balance your hormones, and ignite a lifelong passion for wellness.

The Essence of the Galveston Diet

At its heart, the Galveston Diet focuses on reducing inflammation through a carefully selected array of foods, acknowledging the profound impact that chronic inflammation has on our bodies. Chronic inflammation is a silent antagonist, linked to numerous health issues such as heart disease, diabetes, and autoimmune conditions. It also plays a significant role in weight gain and difficulty in losing weight, especially as we age.

The Galveston Diet is designed to counteract these effects by promoting foods rich in nutrients that naturally combat inflammation. It's not about cutting calories in a dramatic or unsustainable way. Instead, it's about nourishing your body with the right foods that also have the delightful benefit of aiding in weight management and boosting overall vitality.

Why Anti-Inflammatory?

You might wonder why the focus on anti-inflammatory eating. The reason is simple yet profound: inflammation is the root cause of many health issues that plague our society today. By adopting an anti-inflammatory diet, you're not just embarking on a journey to improved physical health; you're also enhancing your mental clarity, energy levels, and emotional well-being.

The foods we advocate in the Galveston Diet are rich in antioxidants, omega-3 fatty acids, fiber, and phytonutrients—all warriors in the battle against inflammation. These nutrients work synergistically to reduce the inflammatory response in the body, protect against oxidative stress, and promote a healthy gut microbiome, which is crucial for overall health.

Hormonal Balance: The Key to Sustainable Weight Management

Another cornerstone of the Galveston Diet is its focus on hormonal balance. Hormones play a pivotal role in regulating metabolism, appetite, and fat storage. As we age, natural changes in hormone levels can make it more challenging to maintain a healthy weight. The Galveston Diet addresses this challenge head-on by including foods that support hormone balance.

For instance, foods high in fiber help regulate insulin levels, while omega-3 fatty acids from fish can improve mood and alleviate symptoms of hormonal fluctuations. Phytoestrogens from soy and flaxseeds can offer natural hormone regulation for those experiencing menopause or other hormonal shifts. By understanding and addressing these hormonal dynamics, the Galveston Diet offers a sustainable approach to weight management and overall health.

The Galveston Plate: A Blueprint for Success

One of the most empowering tools you'll learn in the Galveston Diet is how to build a "Galveston Plate." This simple yet effective blueprint ensures that each meal is balanced, nutritious, and aligned with your health goals. A typical Galveston Plate consists of half non-starchy vegetables, a quarter of lean protein, and a quarter of whole grains or starchy vegetables, with a sprinkling of healthy fats to bring it all together. This method not only simplifies meal planning but also ensures that you're getting a harmonious blend of nutrients at every meal.

Listening to Your Body

A fundamental principle of the Galveston Diet is the importance of listening to your body. This means paying attention to hunger cues, understanding the difference between hunger and cravings, and recognizing how certain foods affect your energy and mood. It's about shifting from a dieting mentality, which often ignores these signals, to a mindful eating approach that honors your body's needs.

The Power of Community

Embarking on the Galveston Diet journey is an exciting step toward better health, but it's also a challenge that requires support, motivation, and encouragement. That's why we emphasize the power of community. Whether it's through social media groups, local meetups, or online forums, connecting with others who are on a similar path can provide invaluable support, share success stories, and offer practical advice.

Your Journey Starts Now

As you begin your journey with the Galveston Diet, remember that this is not a quick fix but a lifestyle change. It's a commitment to treating your body with respect and nourishment. There will be challenges along the way, but the rewards—increased energy, better health, and a deeper understanding of your body—are well worth the effort.

Throughout this subchapter, we've laid the foundation for what the Galveston Diet entails: a focus on anti-inflammatory eating, the importance of hormonal balance, the simplicity of the Galveston Plate, and the transformative power of listening to your body. As you move forward, remember that this journey is unique to you. There is no one-size-fits-all approach to health, and the Galveston Diet is adaptable to meet your individual needs and preferences.

Take this knowledge, embrace the journey, and let the Galveston Diet be your guide to a healthier, happier you. Together, we'll explore the delicious, nourishing world of anti-inflammatory eating and discover how simple, mindful choices can lead to lasting health and wellness. Welcome to the Galveston Diet—your journey to health begins now.

THE SCIENCE BEHIND ANTI-INFLAMMATORY EATING

In the heart of the Galveston Diet lies a compelling narrative that intertwines the wisdom of centuries-old dietary practices with the cutting-edge science of today—anti-inflammatory eating. This approach isn't a fleeting trend but a fundamental shift in how we understand the relationship between food, inflammation, and health. The science behind anti-inflammatory eating is both profound and promising, offering a new lens through which we can view nutrition and wellness.

Unveiling the Role of Inflammation

To appreciate the essence of anti-inflammatory eating, it's essential to first understand what inflammation is. At its most basic, inflammation is the body's natural response to protect itself against harm, including infections, toxins, and injuries. However, when inflammation becomes chronic, it can lead to a myriad of health issues, such as heart disease, arthritis, depression, and cancer. Chronic inflammation is often silent, going undetected for years, and is influenced significantly by lifestyle factors, including diet.

Diet and Inflammation: Connecting the Dots

Numerous studies have highlighted the direct impact our diet has on inflammation levels. Foods high in refined sugars, trans fats, and processed ingredients can trigger an inflammatory response, while whole foods rich in antioxidants, healthy fats, and fiber have the opposite effect, reducing inflammation and promoting health. The Galveston Diet emphasizes the importance of choosing foods that nurture rather than harm, aligning with the body's natural processes to heal and protect itself.

The Anti-Inflammatory Heroes

At the forefront of the Galveston Diet are the anti-inflammatory powerhouses—foods and nutrients that are key players in reducing inflammation:

- **Omega-3 Fatty Acids:** Found in abundance in fatty fish, flaxseeds, and walnuts, omega-3s are celebrated for their anti-inflammatory properties. They help reduce the levels of inflammatory markers in the body, offering protection against a range of diseases.
- **Antioxidants:** Vibrant fruits and vegetables are loaded with antioxidants such as vitamins C and E, carotenoids, and flavonoids. These compounds neutralize free radicals, reducing oxidative stress and inflammation.
- **Fiber:** High-fiber foods like whole grains, legumes, fruits, and vegetables not only keep you full but also play a crucial role in modulating inflammation. They support a healthy gut microbiome, which is linked to reduced inflammation and a stronger immune system.

- **Polyphenols:** Found in green tea, dark chocolate, and red wine, among other foods, polyphenols are compounds that have been shown to reduce inflammation and lower the risk of several diseases.

The Science in Practice: From Theory to Plate

The transition from understanding the science to applying it in daily life is where the Galveston Diet shines. It translates complex nutritional principles into practical, delicious meals that fit seamlessly into your lifestyle. By focusing on whole, nutrient-dense foods and minimizing processed items, the diet naturally aligns with anti-inflammatory principles, making it easier for you to reduce inflammation and improve your health.

A Closer Look at Inflammatory Markers

One-way scientists measure the impact of diet on inflammation is by examining biomarkers in the blood, such as C-reactive protein (CRP), tumor necrosis factor-alpha (TNF-α), and interleukin-6 (IL-6). Research has consistently shown that an anti-inflammatory diet can lower these markers, signaling a reduction in overall inflammation. This evidence underscores the tangible benefits of adopting an anti-inflammatory eating pattern, as promoted by the Galveston Diet.

The Broader Health Implications

The implications of anti-inflammatory eating extend far beyond weight management. By reducing inflammation, you're also lowering your risk of chronic diseases, improving your mood and cognitive function, and enhancing your overall quality of life. The Galveston Diet, with its focus on anti-inflammatory eating, is not just about dieting—it's about choosing a healthier, more vibrant life.

Personalization and Flexibility

A cornerstone of the Galveston Diet's philosophy is the acknowledgment that there is no one-size-fits-all solution to nutrition. The diet encourages personalization, allowing you to adjust your food choices based on your body's responses, preferences, and specific health needs. This flexibility ensures that the anti-inflammatory principles can be integrated into any lifestyle, making sustainable health achievable for everyone.

Empowering Through Education

By understanding the science behind anti-inflammatory eating, you are equipped with the knowledge to make informed decisions about your health. The Galveston Diet is more than a set of guidelines; it's a tool for empowerment, enabling you to take control of your wellness journey with confidence.

Embarking on Your Journey

As you delve into the world of anti-inflammatory eating with the Galveston Diet, remember that each meal is an opportunity to nourish your body and protect your health. The science behind the diet is your guide, illuminating the path to wellness and inspiring you to embrace the transformative power of food. With each bite, you're taking a step towards a healthier, more vibrant you. Welcome to the journey.

HORMONE BALANCE AND ITS ROLE IN OVERALL WELLNESS

In the intricate ballet of our body's systems, hormones play the lead role, orchestrating a wide range of physiological activities that maintain health and wellness. Their influence spans from regulating metabolism and appetite to influencing mood and energy levels. The Galveston Diet shines a spotlight on the critical role of hormone balance, not just for weight management but for overall vitality and well-being. Understanding this relationship is key to harnessing the power of nutrition to support hormonal health.

Hormones: The Body's Chemical Messengers

Hormones are biochemical messengers produced by the endocrine system, working tirelessly to communicate between various parts of the body. Their messages help regulate bodily functions to maintain homeostasis—a state of balance and stability. However, when this delicate balance is disrupted, whether through stress, diet, lifestyle, or environmental factors, it can lead to a cascade of health issues, including weight gain, mood disorders, and chronic diseases.

The Link Between Diet and Hormonal Health

The food we eat plays a pivotal role in influencing hormonal balance. Certain foods can either promote hormonal harmony or contribute to imbalance. For instance, high-glycemic foods can spike insulin levels, leading to an increased risk of insulin resistance, while foods rich in phytoestrogens can mimic estrogen, impacting hormonal health in various ways. The Galveston Diet's emphasis on anti-inflammatory, nutrient-dense foods support the body's natural hormone regulation mechanisms, highlighting the importance of dietary choices in maintaining hormonal balance.

Nutrition and Hormone Regulation

Key components of the Galveston Diet aim to stabilize hormones through targeted nutrition:

- **Fiber:** Consuming high-fiber foods can slow the absorption of sugar into the bloodstream, helping to manage insulin levels and reduce the risk of insulin resistance.

- **Healthy Fats:** Omega-3 fatty acids, found in fish, flaxseeds, and walnuts, play a role in reducing inflammation and can help regulate hormones.
- **Antioxidants:** Foods rich in antioxidants help protect cells from oxidative stress, which can disrupt hormonal balance.
- **Phytonutrients:** Certain plant-based compounds can modulate estrogen levels, offering benefits for hormonal health.

Stress, Cortisol, and Weight

Stress and its hormonal counterpart, cortisol, have a direct impact on weight and health. Cortisol, known as the "stress hormone," can lead to cravings for high-fat, high-sugar foods, contributing to weight gain. The Galveston Diet addresses this issue by promoting foods that help modulate cortisol levels and by emphasizing the importance of managing stress through lifestyle interventions like meditation, exercise, and adequate sleep.

Thyroid Health and Metabolism

The thyroid gland plays a crucial role in regulating metabolism, and its hormones affect nearly every cell in the body. An imbalance in thyroid hormones can lead to symptoms like weight gain, fatigue, and cold sensitivity. The Galveston Diet supports thyroid health by including foods rich in iodine, selenium, and zinc—nutrients essential for thyroid hormone production and metabolism.

Sex Hormones and Weight Management

Sex hormones, including estrogen and testosterone, influence body composition and fat distribution. The Galveston Diet considers the impact of these hormones, offering dietary strategies to support their balance. This includes the incorporation of foods that support liver health and detoxification processes, aiding in the regulation of estrogen metabolism.

The Power of Personalization

Recognizing the unique hormonal landscape of each individual, the Galveston Diet advocates for a personalized approach to nutrition and wellness. By tuning into the body's signals and adjusting dietary choices accordingly, individuals can find the balance that works best for their hormonal health and overall well-being.

A Foundation for Hormonal Harmony

The journey to hormonal balance is multifaceted, involving more than just diet. It encompasses a holistic approach that includes stress management, regular physical activity, adequate sleep, and mindfulness practices. The Galveston Diet serves as a foundation, providing the nutritional building blocks necessary for hormonal health, but it's the integration of these practices that truly supports overall wellness.

Empowering Through Knowledge

Armed with the knowledge of how diet influences hormonal health, you are empowered to make choices that support your body's natural rhythms and processes. The Galveston Diet is more than a nutritional guideline; it's a tool for understanding and nurturing your body, encouraging a harmonious balance that fosters health, vitality, and happiness.

As we conclude this exploration of hormone balance and its role in overall wellness, remember that every step you take towards balancing your hormones through diet and lifestyle is a step towards a healthier, more vibrant you. The Galveston Diet is your companion on this journey, guiding you towards a future where hormonal harmony is not just a goal, but a reality.

CHAPTER 2: SETTING THE FOUNDATION FOR SUCCESS

As we turn the page to Chapter 2, "Setting the Foundation for Success," we delve into the essential groundwork that paves the way for a seamless and fulfilling Galveston Diet journey. Embarking on a lifestyle transformation requires more than just a willingness to change; it necessitates a thoughtful preparation that extends beyond the pantry and into the very fabric of our daily routines. This chapter is designed to equip you with the tools, knowledge, and mindset needed to navigate the path ahead with confidence and ease.

Here, we'll explore the significance of curating a kitchen environment that inspires health and creativity, starting with the essentials—identifying the tools and gadgets that streamline cooking processes and enhance your culinary experience. We'll also guide you through stocking your pantry with anti-inflammatory staples, laying a solid foundation for nutritious and delicious meal creation. Meal planning emerges as a cornerstone strategy for success, offering a roadmap that balances spontaneity with structure. We'll share tips and strategies to demystify meal planning, making it an enjoyable part of your wellness journey rather than a chore. This chapter aims to transform your kitchen from a place of confusion and stress into a sanctuary of health, happiness, and culinary exploration.

As we journey through "Setting the Foundation for Success," remember that the most profound transformations begin with small, intentional steps. This chapter is your first step towards creating a sustainable, joy-filled approach to the Galveston Diet, setting the stage for the vibrant health and wellness that awaits.

KITCHEN ESSENTIALS AND TOOLS FOR YOUR GALVESTON JOURNEY

Embracing the Galveston Diet is not just about changing what you eat; it's about transforming how you prepare, cook, and think about food. The kitchen, often called the heart of the home, plays a pivotal role in this transformation. Equipping it with the right tools and essentials can turn meal preparation from a daunting task into an enjoyable and health-promoting activity. In this subchapter, we'll guide you through setting up your kitchen to support your Galveston journey, ensuring you have everything you need to make nutritious and delicious meals with ease and joy.

High-Quality Knives

A chef is only as good as their knives. Investing in a set of high-quality knives can make a world of difference in your cooking experience. Look for a chef's knife, a paring knife, and a serrated knife as the basics. Sharp, well-crafted knives make chopping vegetables, slicing meats, and mincing herbs effortless, encouraging you to use a variety of fresh ingredients in your Galveston dishes.

Cutting Boards

Consider having multiple cutting boards to prevent cross-contamination between raw meats and vegetables. Opt for bamboo or wood for durability and plastic for easy cleaning. Keeping your boards organized and in good condition is essential for food safety and efficiency in the kitchen.

Blender or Food Processor

A high-powered blender or food processor is invaluable for the Galveston Diet, allowing you to whip up smoothies, soups, sauces, and even nut butters with minimal effort. These tools open up a world of possibilities for incorporating a variety of anti-inflammatory foods into your diet in creative and delicious ways.

Measuring Cups and Spoons

Accuracy in measuring ingredients can impact the success of a recipe, especially when baking. Measuring cups and spoons are indispensable for following recipes accurately and making adjustments to suit your dietary needs. Look for durable, easy-to-read sets that can go in the dishwasher for easy cleanup.

Mixing Bowls

A set of mixing bowls in various sizes will serve you well for everything from tossing salads to mixing batter. Opt for bowls that nest within each other to save space. Materials like stainless steel or glass are preferred for their durability and ease of cleaning.

Cookware and Bakeware

Investing in quality cookware and bakeware sets the stage for successful Galveston meals. Look for non-stick frying pans, saucepans, and a sturdy baking sheet as the foundation. Cast iron skillets are excellent for their heat retention and versatility, while a good-quality baking dish is essential for casseroles and roasted vegetables.

Storage Containers

Prepping meals in advance is a cornerstone of the Galveston Diet, and having a variety of storage containers makes this process streamlined and practical. Glass containers with airtight lids are ideal for storing leftovers, prepped ingredients, and ready-to-eat meals, keeping them fresh and making mealtime convenient.

Herb and Spice Grinder

Fresh herbs and spices are at the heart of anti-inflammatory cooking, offering not only health benefits but also vibrant flavors. An herb grinder or a mortar and pestle set allow you to grind fresh spices and herbs, enhancing the taste and nutritional value of your meals.

Digital Scale

A digital kitchen scale can be a game-changer for those serious about portion control and accuracy in ingredient measurement. It ensures you're using the exact amounts required in recipes, which is particularly important for maintaining the balance of nutrients advocated in the Galveston Diet.

Spiralizer

Introducing more vegetables into your diet in fun and interesting ways can be made easy with a spiralizer. This tool transforms vegetables like zucchini, carrots, and sweet potatoes into noodles, adding a new dimension to salads, stir-fries, and pasta dishes, aligning with the Galveston Diet's emphasis on plant-based, nutrient-rich foods.

Slow Cooker or Instant Pot

For busy individuals looking to adhere to the Galveston Diet, a slow cooker or an Instant Pot can be a lifesaver. These devices allow for easy, hands-off cooking, making it possible to come home to a warm, healthy meal that's ready to eat. They're perfect for soups, stews, and other one-pot dishes that can be prepared in advance and enjoyed throughout the week.

Setting the Stage for Success

Equipping your kitchen with these essentials is more than just about having the right tools; it's about creating an environment that inspires and supports your commitment to health and wellness. Each item is a building block in the foundation of your Galveston journey, designed to make the process of preparing and enjoying nutritious meals not just simple, but a pleasure. With your kitchen set up for success, you're one step closer to achieving the vibrant health and vitality that comes with embracing the Galveston Diet.

STOCKING YOUR PANTRY WITH ANTI-INFLAMMATORY STAPLES

Navigating the Galveston Diet begins with a fundamental step: transforming your pantry into a haven of anti-inflammatory staples. This preparation sets the stage for success, ensuring that the building blocks for nutritious, healing meals are always within reach. The key to a well-stocked pantry is diversity—a variety of flavors, textures, and nutrients that not only cater to your health needs but also ignite your culinary creativity. Here, we delve into the essentials that form the backbone of the Galveston Diet pantry, empowering you to craft meals that nourish and delight.

Whole Grains: The Fiber Foundation

Whole grains are a cornerstone of the anti-inflammatory pantry, rich in fiber, which is essential for gut health and inflammation control. Quinoa, brown rice, oats, and barley not only provide a hearty base for meals but also contribute to satiety and blood sugar stabilization. These grains can be the starting point for a myriad of dishes, from morning porridges to savory dinner bowls.

Legumes: Plant-Based Protein Powerhouses

Beans and lentils are not just versatile and delicious; they're also packed with protein, fiber, and key nutrients like iron and potassium. Incorporating a variety of legumes into your diet supports heart health and provides a satisfying, plant-based protein source for salads, soups, and stews.

Nuts and Seeds: Nutrient-Dense Snacks

Almonds, walnuts, chia seeds, and flaxseeds are small but mighty sources of omega-3 fatty acids, antioxidants, and healthy fats. They add crunch and nutrition to breakfasts, salads, and snacks, while their anti-inflammatory properties support overall wellness.

Healthy Oils: Essential Fats for Flavor and Function

Olive oil and avocado oil are staples in the anti-inflammatory kitchen, celebrated for their heart-healthy fats and ability to enhance the absorption of fat-soluble vitamins. These oils are perfect for dressings, sautéing, and drizzling over dishes to add richness and depth of flavor.

Herbs and Spices: The Anti-Inflammatory Arsenal

Turmeric, ginger, garlic, cinnamon, and rosemary not only elevate the taste of any dish but also boast powerful anti-inflammatory benefits. Keeping a well-stocked spice rack encourages culinary experimentation while maximizing the healing potential of your meals.

Canned Goods: Convenience Meets Nutrition

Canned tomatoes, pumpkin, and coconut milk are pantry essentials that offer convenience without compromising on nutrition. They serve as the base for soups, curries, and sauces, providing depth of flavor and a wealth of nutrients. Opt for low-sodium options and BPA-free cans to ensure quality and healthfulness.

Vinegars and Citrus: Brightness in Every Drop

Apple cider vinegar, balsamic vinegar, and a variety of citrus fruits like lemons and limes can transform any meal with a burst of flavor. Beyond their culinary uses, these ingredients help balance blood sugar levels and add a refreshing zest to dressings, marinades, and beverages.

Sweeteners: Natural Choices for a Hint of Sweetness

In the Galveston Diet, refined sugars are replaced with natural sweeteners like honey, maple syrup, and dates. These options provide a touch of sweetness in moderation, complementing the flavors of your dishes without spiking your blood sugar.

Whole Food Snacks: Ready-to-Eat Wholesomeness

For those moments when you need a quick bite, having whole food snacks like dried fruits, unsweetened applesauce, and roasted chickpeas ensures you have healthy options at hand. These snacks provide essential nutrients and energy without the added sugars and unhealthy fats found in processed snacks.

Teas and Hydration Helpers

Green tea, herbal teas, and infused water ingredients like cucumber and mint support hydration while offering antioxidant benefits. Keeping these items in your pantry encourages regular hydration, an often-overlooked aspect of anti-inflammatory living.

Building Your Anti-Inflammatory Pantry

Creating an anti-inflammatory pantry is a dynamic process that evolves with your dietary preferences, cooking habits, and nutritional needs. Start with these essentials, and allow your pantry to grow and change as you discover new ingredients, recipes, and flavors that align with the Galveston Diet's principles. Remember, the goal is not just to follow a diet but to embark on a journey of wellness, where food becomes a source of healing, energy, and joy.

The Path Forward

With your pantry now stocked with anti-inflammatory staples, you're well-equipped to tackle the Galveston Diet with confidence and creativity. These ingredients are the building blocks for meals that not only taste delicious but also support your health goals, making every bite a step towards a more vibrant, balanced life. As you move forward, let your pantry inspire you to explore new recipes, experiment with flavors, and enjoy the process of nourishing your body and soul.

MEAL PLANNING MADE EASY: TIPS AND STRATEGIES FOR SUCCESS

Embarking on the Galveston Diet journey, while enriching, can seem daunting at first glance. The key to seamlessly integrating this healthful way of eating into your busy life is through effective meal planning. This isn't about stringent schedules or depriving yourself of the foods you love; it's about creating a flexible structure that supports your health goals, saves time, and reduces stress. Here, we unveil a treasure trove of tips and strategies designed to make meal planning not just easy but enjoyable.

Start with a Vision

Begin each week with a vision of what you want to achieve. Whether it's incorporating more anti-inflammatory foods into your diet, trying new recipes, or simply ensuring you have healthful meals prepared for busy nights, setting clear intentions will guide your meal planning process.

Keep It Simple

Simplicity is your ally. Choose recipes that don't require extensive preparation or C. T.s. Dishes that can be made in large batches, like soups, stews, and casseroles, are perfect for meal planning. They save time and ensure you have multiple meals from a single cooking session.

Plan for Variety

To keep your diet interesting and balanced, incorporate a variety of proteins, vegetables, and grains throughout the week. This not only prevents dietary boredom but also ensures you're getting a wide range of nutrients. Rotate your favorites and be open to trying new ingredients to keep your meals exciting and diverse.

Make a List and Shop Smart

Armed with your meal plan, create a shopping list of the ingredients you'll need. Organize your list by category (produce, proteins, pantry items) to streamline your shopping trip. Stick to your list to avoid impulse buys that don't align with your health goals. Whenever possible, opt for fresh, local, and seasonal ingredients to maximize nutrition and flavor.

Batch Cooking and Prep

Dedicate a few hours each week to batch cooking and prepping ingredients. Cook grains and legumes, roast vegetables, and prepare proteins in advance. Having these components ready to go makes assembling meals throughout the week quick and effortless. Store prepped ingredients in clear containers in the fridge for easy access.

Embrace Leftovers

Plan for meals that can easily be repurposed into new dishes. For example, roasted chicken can become a salad topping, a stir-fry ingredient, or a filling for wraps. Viewing leftovers as a base for new creations reduces waste and maximizes your cooking efforts.

Flexible Meal Templates

Instead of rigid recipes, consider using flexible meal templates. For instance, designate one night a week for stir-fries, where you can mix and match proteins and vegetables based on what you have on hand. This approach allows for creativity and adaptation to last-minute changes in your schedule or inventory.

Involve Your Household

Meal planning and preparation can be a shared activity. Involve your family or housemates in the process, from selecting recipes to cooking together. This not only divides the workload but also enhances the dining experience, making meals a time for connection and enjoyment.

Use Technology to Your Advantage

Leverage meal planning apps and online resources to streamline the process. Many apps offer features like recipe organization, automated shopping lists, and meal reminders, simplifying the planning process and keeping you on track.

Reflect and Adjust

At the end of each week, take time to reflect on what worked well and what didn't. Did you find yourself with too many leftovers? Were there nights when cooking felt like a chore? Use these insights to adjust your meal planning strategy for the following week, continually refining the process to better suit your needs and lifestyle.

Celebrate Your Successes

Finally, celebrate the wins, no matter how small. Successfully preparing a week's worth of healthy meals, trying a new recipe that becomes a family favorite, or simply feeling more energized and less stressed about mealtime are all achievements worth acknowledging. Celebrate these moments and let them motivate you as you continue on your Galveston Diet journey.

Meal planning is an art that evolves with practice, patience, and persistence. By embracing these tips and strategies, you'll discover that eating healthfully and following the Galveston Diet can be not just manageable but truly rewarding. Here's to setting the foundation for success—one meal at a time.

CHAPTER 3: BREAKFASTS TO ENERGIZE YOUR DAY

Embarking on each new day with vitality and clarity sets the tone for success and wellness. In "Breakfasts to Energize Your Day," we explore the foundational role of the first meal in igniting your metabolic engine and fueling your body with nourishing, anti-inflammatory ingredients that align with the Galveston Diet principles. This chapter isn't just about recipes; it's an invitation to redefine breakfast as a cherished ritual that supports your health goals and satisfies your palate.

Gone are the days of sugary cereals and hurried, nutritionally void snacks. Here, we introduce you to a variety of breakfast options designed to provide sustained energy, optimize hormone balance, and reduce inflammation. From savory dishes rich in protein and healthy fats to sweet, fiber-packed delights, these recipes are curated to make your first meal the most anticipated part of your morning. Understanding the importance of convenience for your busy lifestyle, we've also included quick and easy options that don't compromise on nutrition or taste. Whether you have a leisurely morning or are on-the-go, you'll find recipes that fit seamlessly into your routine, ensuring that no matter how hectic your day, it starts on a nourishing note.

As you delve into this chapter, allow the promise of delicious, healthful breakfasts to inspire your mornings. These meals are more than just food on a plate; they're a daily reaffirmation of your commitment to living well, energizing your body and mind for the adventures that lie ahead.

BLUEBERRY WALNUT SMOOTHIE BOWL

PREP.T.: 5 min **C. T.:** 0 min

MODE OF COOKING: Blending - **SERVINGS:** 1

INGREDIENTS: One cup frozen blueberries, one banana, half a cup spinach, half a cup almond milk, two tablespoons of walnuts, one tablespoon chia seeds, and one teaspoon honey.

DIRECTIONS: Blend blueberries, banana, spinach, and almond milk until smooth. Top with walnuts, chia seeds, together with a honey drizzle.

N.V.: Calories: 310, Fat: 15 g, 44 g of carbohydrates, 6 g of protein, 24 g of sugar, 80 mg of sodium, 600 mg of potassium, and 0 mg of cholesterol.

CHIA SEED PUDDING WITH MIXED BERRIES

PREP.T.: 5 min (plus overnight refrigeration) **C. T.:** 0 min

MODE OF COOKING: Refrigeration - **SERVINGS:** 2

INGREDIENTS: Chia seeds, 1/4 cup; Coconut milk, 1 cup; Mixed berries, 1/2 cup; Maple syrup, 1 Tbsp.; Vanilla extract, 1/2 tsp.

DIRECTIONS: Mix chia seeds with coconut milk, maple syrup, and vanilla. Refrigerate overnight. Top with berries before serving.

N.V.: Calories: 280, Fat: 18 g, Carbohydrates: 24 g, Protein: 5 g, Sugar: 12 g, Sodium: 15 mg, Potassium: 200 mg, Cholesterol: 0 mg.

SWEET POTATO AND BLACK BEAN BREAKFAST BURRITO

PREP.T.: 10 min **C. T.:** 20 min

MODE OF COOKING: Sauteing - **SERVINGS:** 4

INGREDIENTS: Sweet potatoes, 2 cups; Black beans, 1 cup; Eggs, 4; Whole wheat tortillas, 4; Avocado, 1; Salsa, 1/2 cup; Cumin, 1 tsp; Olive oil, 1 Tbsp.; Salt and pepper to taste.

DIRECTIONS: Sauté sweet potatoes in oil, cumin, salt, pepper until tender. Add beans, scramble in eggs. Fill tortillas, top with avocado, salsa.

N.V.: Calories: 350, Fat: 15 g, Carbohydrates: 45 g, Protein: 15 g, Sugar: 5 g, Sodium: 600 mg, Potassium: 800 mg, Cholesterol: 185 mg.

GREEN GODDESS SMOOTHIE

PREP.T.: 5 min **C. T.:** 0 min

MODE OF COOKING: Blending - **SERVINGS:** 1

INGREDIENTS: Spinach, 1 cup; Avocado, 1/2; Green apple, 1; Celery, 1 stalk; Lemon juice, 1 Tbsp.; Ginger, 1 tsp; Water, 1 cup.

DIRECTIONS: Blend all ingredients until smooth. Add water to adjust consistency.

N.V.: Calories: 220, Fat: 11 g, Carbohydrates: 30 g, Protein: 3 g, Sugar: 15 g, Sodium: 70 mg, Potassium: 890 mg, Cholesterol: 0 mg.

QUINOA BREAKFAST BOWL

PREP.T.: 5 min **C. T.:** 15 min

MODE OF COOKING: Boiling - **SERVINGS:** 2

INGREDIENTS: Quinoa, 1 cup; Almond milk, 2 cups; Cinnamon, 1 tsp; Apple, 1 diced; Walnuts, 1/4 cup; Honey, 2 Tbsp.

DIRECTIONS: Cook quinoa in almond milk, cinnamon. Stir in apple during last 5 min. Top with walnuts, honey.

N.V.: Calories: 330, Fat: 9 g, 55 g of carbohydrates, 8 g of protein, 20 g of sugar, 80 mg of sodium, 400 mg of potassium, and 0 mg of cholesterol.

EGG MUFFINS WITH SPINACH AND FETA

PREP.T.: 10 min **C. T.:** 20 min

MODE OF COOKING: Baking - **SERVINGS:** 6

INGREDIENTS: Eggs, 6; Spinach, 1 cup chopped; Feta cheese, 1/2 cup crumbled; Milk, 1/4 cup; Salt and pepper to taste.

DIRECTIONS: Whisk eggs, milk, salt, pepper. Stir in spinach, feta. Pour into muffin tins. Bake at 350°F (177°C) until set.

N.V.: Calories: 140, Fat: 9 g, Carbohydrates: 2 g, Protein: 12 g, Sugar: 1 g, Sodium: 320 mg, Potassium: 150 mg, Cholesterol: 190 mg.

ALMOND BUTTER AND BANANA OPEN SANDWICH

PREP.T.: 5 min **C. T.:** 0 min

MODE OF COOKING: Assembling - **SERVINGS:** 1

INGREDIENTS: Whole grain bread, 1 slice; Almond butter, 2 Tbsp.; Banana, 1 sliced; Chia seeds, 1 tsp; Honey, 1 tsp.

DIRECTIONS: Spread almond butter on toast, top with banana slices. Sprinkle with chia seeds, drizzle with honey.

N.V.: Calories: 330, Fat: 16 g, Carbohydrates: 44 g, Protein: 8 g, Sugar: 20 g, Sodium: 200 mg, Potassium: 400 mg, Cholesterol: 0 mg.

TURMERIC GINGER OATMEAL

PREP.T.: 5 min **C. T.:** 10 min **MODE OF COOKING:** Boiling - **SERVINGS:** 2

INGREDIENTS: Rolled oats, 1 cup; Water, 2 cups; Turmeric, 1/2 tsp; Ginger, 1 tsp; Honey, 1 Tbsp.; Almond milk, 1/2 cup; Almonds, 1/4 cup; Salt, a pinch.

DIRECTIONS: Combine oats, water, turmeric, ginger, and salt; boil. Simmer until creamy. Stir in almond milk, top with honey and almonds.

N.V.: Calories: 220, Fat: 6 g, Carbohydrates: 36 g, Protein: 6 g, Sugar: 9 g, Sodium: 60 mg, Potassium: 200 mg, Cholesterol: 0 mg.

AVOCADO TOAST WITH POACHED EGG

PREP.T.: 5 min **C. T.:** 10 min **MODE OF COOKING:** Poaching/Toasting - **SERVINGS:** 1

INGREDIENTS: Whole grain bread, 1 slice; Avocado, 1/2; Egg, 1; Lemon juice, 1 tsp; Red pepper flakes, a pinch; Salt and pepper to taste.

DIRECTIONS: Toast bread, mash avocado on top with lemon juice, salt, pepper. Poach egg, place on avocado toast, sprinkle with red pepper flakes.

N.V.: Calories: 300, Fat: 20 g, Carbohydrates: 23 g, Protein: 12 g, Sugar: 3 g, Sodium: 210 mg, Potassium: 500 mg, Cholesterol: 185 mg.

GREEN GODDESS SMOOTHIE

PREP.T.: 5 min **C. T.:** 0 min **MODE OF COOKING:** Blending - **SERVINGS:** 1

INGREDIENTS: Spinach, 1 cup; Avocado, 1/2; Green apple, 1; Celery, 1 stalk; Lemon juice, 1 Tbsp.; Ginger, 1 tsp; Water, 1 cup.

DIRECTIONS: Blend all ingredients until smooth. Add water to adjust consistency.

N.V.: Calories: 220, Fat: 11 g, Carbohydrates: 30 g, Protein: 3 g, Sugar: 15 g, Sodium: 70 mg, Potassium: 890 mg, Cholesterol: 0 mg.

COTTAGE CHEESE AND PEACH PARFAIT

PREP.T.: 5 min **C. T.:** 0 min **MODE OF COOKING:** Layering - **SERVINGS:** 1

INGREDIENTS: Cottage cheese, 1 cup; Peaches, 1 cup sliced; Granola, 1/4 cup; Honey, 1 Tbsp.; Almonds, 2 Tbsp. sliced.

DIRECTIONS: Layer cottage cheese, peaches, granola in a glass. Top with almonds, drizzle with honey.

N.V.: Calories: 240, Fat: 10 g, Carbohydrates: 30 g, Protein: 10 g, Sugar: 4 g, Sodium: 200 mg, Potassium: 600 mg, Cholesterol: 25 mg.

VEGAN SWEET POTATO AND BLACK BEAN CHILI

PREP.T.: 15 min **C. T.:** 30 min **MODE OF COOKING:** Simmering - **SERVINGS:** 4

INGREDIENTS: Sweet potatoes, 2 cups (cubed); Black beans, 2 cups (drained); Diced tomatoes, 2 cups; Onion, 1 (chopped); Garlic, 2 tsp (minced); Chili powder, 2 tsp; Cumin, 1 tsp; Vegetable broth, 4 cups; Olive oil, 1 Tbsp.; Salt and pepper to taste; Cilantro, 1/4 cup (chopped) for garnish.

DIRECTIONS: Sauté onion, garlic in oil; Add sweet potatoes, spices, cook 5 min; Add beans, tomatoes, broth; Simmer until potatoes are tender; Garnish with cilantro.

N.V.: Calories: 250, Fat: 5 g, Carbohydrates: 45 g, Protein: 10 g, Sugar: 8 g, Sodium: 300 mg, Potassium: 900 mg, Cholesterol: 0 mg.

GARLIC HERB ROASTED CHICKEN WITH VEGETABLES

PREP.T.: 20 min **C. T.:** 60 min **MODE OF COOKING:** Roasting - **SERVINGS:** 4

INGREDIENTS: Chicken, 1 whole (about 4 lbs); Carrots, 1 cup (sliced); Potatoes, 2 cups (cubed); Onion, 1 (quartered); Garlic, 4 cloves (minced); Olive oil, 3 Tbsp.; Rosemary, 1 Tbsp. (chopped); Thyme, 1 tsp; Salt and pepper to taste.

DIRECTIONS: Rub chicken with oil, herbs, garlic, salt, pepper; Surround with vegetables; Roast at 425°F (220°C) until chicken is cooked through.

N.V.: Calories: 420, Fat: 24 g, Carbohydrates: 22 g, Protein: 32 g, Sugar: 3 g, Sodium: 200 mg, Potassium: 800 mg, Cholesterol: 105 mg.

PARMESAN ZUCCHINI AND CORN

PREP.T.: 10 min **C. T.:** 10 min **MODE OF COOKING:** Sautéing - **SERVINGS:** 4

INGREDIENTS: Zucchini, 2 cups (sliced); Corn, 1 cup; Parmesan cheese, 1/2 cup (grated); Garlic, 1 tsp (minced); Olive oil, 1 Tbsp.; Basil, 1 Tbsp. (chopped); Salt and pepper to taste.

DIRECTIONS: Sauté garlic in oil; Add zucchini, corn, cook until tender; Stir in Parmesan, basil; Season with salt, pepper.

N.V.: Calories: 150, Fat: 8 g, Carbohydrates: 15 g, Protein: 7 g, Sugar: 4 g, Sodium: 150 mg, Potassium: 300 mg, Cholesterol: 11 mg.

CHAPTER 4: SATISFYING LUNCHES FOR BUSY DAYS

In the hustle and bustle of daily life, finding the time to prepare a nutritious lunch can often fall by the wayside, leading us to quick fixes that may not align with our health goals. "Satisfying Lunches for Busy Days" is designed to bridge that gap, offering a collection of recipes that are not only quick and easy to prepare but also deeply nourishing, keeping you energized and focused through the afternoon slump.

These recipes are crafted with the principles of the Galveston Diet in mind, emphasizing anti-inflammatory ingredients, balanced macronutrients, and, above all, simplicity and flavor. From vibrant salads packed with a rainbow of nutrients to hearty soups that can be prepared ahead of time and enjoyed throughout the week, each recipe is a building block towards maintaining a balanced diet in the midst of a busy schedule.

We understand that lunch is often eaten in the midst of multitasking, whether it be at your desk, in a quick break between meetings, or on the go. Thus, we've focused on meals that are not only quick to assemble but also portable and enjoyable, even when time is of the essence. These lunches are designed to be prepared in advance, requiring minimal last-minute prep, so you can grab, go, and know you're fueling your body with the best.

Embark on this chapter as your guide to transforming your midday meal from an afterthought to a moment of nourishment and pleasure, even on your busiest days. Let's redefine what a quick lunch can be, turning it into a highlight of your day that supports your journey towards optimal health and vitality.

SPINACH AND QUINOA SALAD WITH LEMON VINAIGRETTE

PREP.T.: 10 min **C. T.:** 15 min **MODE OF COOKING:** Boiling - **SERVINGS:** 4

INGREDIENTS: Quinoa, 1 cup; Spinach, 2 cups; Cherry tomatoes, 1 cup; Cucumber, 1 cup diced; Feta cheese, 1/2 cup; Olive oil, 3 Tbsp.; Lemon juice, 2 Tbsp.; Salt and pepper to taste.

DIRECTIONS: Cook quinoa, let cool. Toss with vegetables, cheese. Whisk oil, lemon juice, salt, pepper for dressing. Combine.

N.V.: Calories: 250, Fat: 15 g, Carbohydrates: 22 g, Protein: 8 g, Sugar: 3 g, Sodium: 200 mg, Potassium: 300 mg, Cholesterol: 25 mg.

TURKEY AVOCADO WRAP

PREP.T.: 5 min **C. T.:** 0 min **MODE OF COOKING:** Wrapping - **SERVINGS:** 2

INGREDIENTS: Whole wheat tortillas, 2; Turkey breast slices, 4 oz; Avocado, 1 mashed; Romaine lettuce, 1 cup; Mustard, 1 Tbsp.; Salt and pepper to taste.

DIRECTIONS: Spread avocado on tortillas, add turkey, lettuce, mustard. Season, roll tightly.

N.V.: Calories: 320, Fat: 15 g, Carbohydrates: 27 g, Protein: 20 g, Sugar: 2 g, Sodium: 400 mg, Potassium: 500 mg, Cholesterol: 50 mg.

MEDITERRANEAN LENTIL SALAD

PREP.T.: 15 min **C. T.:** 20 min **MODE OF COOKING:** Boiling - **SERVINGS:** 4

INGREDIENTS: Lentils, 1 cup; Cherry tomatoes, 1 cup halved; Cucumber, 1 cup diced; Red onion, 1/4 cup diced; Feta cheese, 1/2 cup; Olive oil, 3 Tbsp.; Lemon juice, 2 Tbsp.; Salt and pepper to taste.

DIRECTIONS: Cook lentils, cool. Mix with vegetables, cheese. Dress with oil, lemon juice. Season.

N.V.: Calories: 280, Fat: 14 g, Carbohydrates: 30 g, Protein: 12 g, Sugar: 4 g, Sodium: 200 mg, Potassium: 400 mg, Cholesterol: 25 mg.

CHICKPEA SALAD SANDWICH

PREP.T.: 10 min **C. T.:** 0 min **MODE OF COOKING:** Mashing - **SERVINGS:** 2

INGREDIENTS: Chickpeas, 1 cup mashed; Celery, 1/2 cup diced; Onion, 1/4 cup diced; Mayonnaise, 2 Tbsp.; Dijon mustard, 1 tsp; Whole grain bread, 4 slices; Lettuce leaves, 4; Salt and pepper to taste.

DIRECTIONS: Mix chickpeas, celery, onion, mayonnaise, mustard. Season. Spread on bread, add lettuce.

N.V.: Calories: 350, Fat: 9 g, Carbohydrates: 52 g, Protein: 12 g, Sugar: 5 g, Sodium: 600 mg, Potassium: 300 mg, Cholesterol: 5 mg.

SOBA NOODLE AND EDAMAME BOWL

PREP.T.: 10 min **C. T.:** 5 min **MODE OF COOKING:** Boiling - **SERVINGS:** 4

INGREDIENTS: Soba noodles, 8 oz; Edamame, 1 cup shelled; Carrots, 1 cup julienned; Cabbage, 1 cup shredded; Soy sauce, 3 Tbsp.; Sesame oil, 1 Tbsp.; Ginger, 1 tsp grated; Sesame seeds, 1 tsp; Salt to taste.

DIRECTIONS: Cook noodles, edamame. Toss with vegetables, sauce. Top with sesame seeds.

N.V.: Calories: 290, Fat: 7 g, Carbohydrates: 45 g, Protein: 12 g, Sugar: 3 g, Sodium: 630 mg, Potassium: 400 mg, Cholesterol: 0 mg.

ROASTED VEGETABLE AND HUMMUS PITA

PREP.T.: 15 min **C. T.:** 20 min **MODE OF COOKING:** Roasting - **SERVINGS:** 4

INGREDIENTS: Zucchini, 1 cup sliced; Bell peppers, 1 cup sliced; Red onion, 1 cup sliced; Hummus, 1 cup; Whole wheat pita bread, 4; Olive oil, 2 Tbsp.; Salt and pepper to taste.

DIRECTIONS: Roast vegetables with oil, salt, pepper. Fill pita with hummus, vegetables.

N.V.: Calories: 310, Fat: 9 g, Carbohydrates: 49 g, Protein: 9 g, Sugar: 5 g, Sodium: 400 mg, Potassium: 300 mg, Cholesterol: 0 mg.

SMOKED SALMON AND CREAM CHEESE BAGEL

PREP.T.: 5 min **C. T.:** 0 min **MODE OF COOKING:** Assembling - **SERVINGS:** 2

INGREDIENTS: Whole grain bagels, 2; Smoked salmon, 4 oz; Cream cheese, 2 Tbsp.; Capers, 1 Tbsp.; Red onion, 1/4 cup thinly sliced; Dill, 1 tsp chopped; Lemon wedges, for serving.

DIRECTIONS: Spread cream cheese on bagels, top with salmon, onion, capers, dill. Serve with lemon.

N.V.: Calories: 370, Fat: 12 g, Carbohydrates: 45 g, Protein: 22 g, Sugar: 6 g, Sodium: 710 mg, Potassium: 200 mg, Cholesterol: 30 mg.

SPICY THAI PEANUT CHICKEN WRAP

PREP.T.: 10 min **C. T.:** 0 min **MODE OF COOKING:** Wrapping - **SERVINGS:** 2

INGREDIENTS: Cooked chicken breast, 1 cup shredded; Whole wheat tortillas, 2; Carrots, 1/2 cup grated; Cucumber, 1/2 cup sliced; Peanut sauce, 3 Tbsp.; Cilantro, 1/4 cup; Salt and pepper to taste.

DIRECTIONS: Toss chicken with peanut sauce, vegetables. Fill tortillas, roll.

N.V.: Calories: 320, Fat: 12 g, Carbohydrates: 30 g, Protein: 25 g, Sugar: 5 g, Sodium: 600 mg, Potassium: 300 mg, Cholesterol: 60 mg.

GRILLED VEGETABLE QUINOA SALAD

PREP.T.: 15 min **C. T.:** 10 min **MODE OF COOKING:** Grilling - **SERVINGS:** 4

INGREDIENTS: Quinoa, 1 cup cooked; Zucchini, 1 cup sliced; Eggplant, 1 cup sliced; Red bell pepper, 1 cup sliced; Olive oil, 2 Tbsp.; Lemon juice, 2 Tbsp.; Feta cheese, 1/2 cup; Salt and pepper to taste.

DIRECTIONS: Grill vegetables, mix with quinoa, lemon juice, oil. Top with feta.

N.V.: Calories: 280, Fat: 14 g, Carbohydrates: 30 g, Protein: 8 g, Sugar: 4 g, Sodium: 200 mg, Potassium: 450 mg, Cholesterol: 25 mg.

CAULIFLOWER BUFFALO WRAPS

PREP.T.: 10 min **C. T.:** 20 min **MODE OF COOKING:** Baking - **SERVINGS:** 4

INGREDIENTS: Cauliflower, 2 cups florets; Whole wheat tortillas, 4; Hot sauce, 1/4 cup; Greek yogurt, 1 cup; Garlic powder, 1 tsp; Lettuce, 1 cup shredded; Carrots, 1/2 cup shredded; Celery, 1/2 cup diced; Salt and pepper to taste.

DIRECTIONS: Toss cauliflower in hot sauce, bake. Mix yogurt, garlic. Fill tortillas with cauliflower, yogurt, vegetables.

N.V.: Calories: 220, Fat: 6 g, Carbohydrates: 34 g, Protein: 12 g, Sugar: 5 g, Sodium: 700 mg, Potassium: 400 mg, Cholesterol: 5 mg.

POMEGRANATE CHICKEN SALAD

PREP.T.: 15 min **C. T.:** 0 min **MODE OF COOKING:** Mixing - **SERVINGS:** 4

INGREDIENTS: Cooked chicken breast, 1 cup chopped; Mixed greens, 4 cups; Pomegranate seeds, 1/2 cup; Avocado, 1 diced; Almonds, 1/4 cup sliced; Olive oil, 3 Tbsp.; Balsamic vinegar, 1 Tbsp.; Honey, 1 tsp; Salt and pepper to taste.

DIRECTIONS: Combine all ingredients in a large bowl. Drizzle with dressing made from oil, vinegar, and honey. Toss gently.

N.V.: Calories: 290, Fat: 19 g, Carbohydrates: 15 g, Protein: 17 g, Sugar: 7 g, Sodium: 150 mg, Potassium: 400 mg, Cholesterol: 40 mg.

AVOCADO QUINOA STUFFED TOMATOES

PREP.T.: 20 min **C. T.:** 0 min **MODE OF COOKING:** Assembling - **SERVINGS:** 4

INGREDIENTS: Large tomatoes, 4 halved; Quinoa, 1 cup cooked; Avocado, 1 diced; Cucumber, 1/2 cup diced; Feta cheese, 1/4 cup crumbled; Lemon juice, 2 Tbsp.; Olive oil, 1 Tbsp.; Salt and pepper to taste.

DIRECTIONS: Hollow out tomatoes. Mix quinoa, avocado, cucumber, cheese, lemon juice, oil. Stuff tomatoes. Season.

N.V.: Calories: 250, Fat: 14 g, Carbohydrates: 27 g, Protein: 7 g, Sugar: 4 g, Sodium: 200 mg, Potassium: 450 mg, Cholesterol: 15 mg.

TUNA AND BEAN SALAD

PREP.T.: 10 min **C. T.:** 0 min **MODE OF COOKING:** Mixing - **SERVINGS:** 4

INGREDIENTS: Canned tuna, 2 cans drained; White beans, 1 cup; Red onion, 1/4 cup finely chopped; Parsley, 1/4 cup chopped; Olive oil, 3 Tbsp.; Lemon juice, 2 Tbsp.; Salt and pepper to taste.

DIRECTIONS: In a bowl, mix tuna, beans, onion, parsley. Dress with olive oil and lemon juice. Season.

N.V.: Calories: 220, Fat: 8 g, Carbohydrates: 18 g, Protein: 20 g, Sugar: 2 g, Sodium: 300 mg, Potassium: 400 mg, Cholesterol: 30 mg.

EGGPLANT CAPRESE SANDWICH

PREP.T.: 10 min **C. T.:** 5 min **MODE OF COOKING:** Grilling - **SERVINGS:** 2

INGREDIENTS: Eggplant, 1 large sliced; Fresh mozzarella, 4 oz sliced; Tomato, 1 sliced; Basil leaves, 1/4 cup; Balsamic glaze, 1 Tbsp.; Olive oil, for brushing; Salt and pepper to taste.

DIRECTIONS: Brush eggplant with oil, grill until tender. Layer eggplant, mozzarella, tomato, basil on bread. Drizzle with glaze.

N.V.: Calories: 320, Fat: 18 g, Carbohydrates: 27 g, Protein: 16 g, Sugar: 8 g, Sodium: 400 mg, Potassium: 300 mg, Cholesterol: 45 mg.

SPICY TURKEY LETTUCE WRAPS

PREP.T.: 15 min **C. T.:** 10 min **MODE OF COOKING:** Sautéing - **SERVINGS:** 4

INGREDIENTS: Ground turkey, 1 lb; Lettuce leaves, 8 (large); Onion, 1/2 cup diced; Garlic, 1 tsp minced; Soy sauce, 2 Tbsp.; Hoisin sauce, 1 Tbsp.; Ginger, 1 tsp grated; Sriracha, 1 tsp; Olive oil, 1 Tbsp.; Water chestnuts, 1/2 cup diced.

DIRECTIONS: Sauté onion, garlic in oil. Add turkey, cook. Stir in sauces, ginger, water chestnuts. Serve in lettuce.

N.V.: Calories: 230, Fat: 10 g, Carbohydrates: 12 g, Protein: 24 g, Sugar: 5 g, Sodium: 600 mg, Potassium: 300 mg, Cholesterol: 60 mg.

BEETROOT AND GOAT CHEESE SALAD

PREP.T.: 10 min **C. T.:** 0 min **MODE OF COOKING:** Mixing - **SERVINGS:** 4

INGREDIENTS: Mixed greens, 4 cups; Cooked beetroot, 1 cup diced; Goat cheese, 1/2 cup crumbled; Walnuts, 1/4 cup toasted; Olive oil, 2 Tbsp.; Balsamic vinegar, 1 Tbsp.; Honey, 1 tsp; Salt and pepper to taste.

DIRECTIONS: Toss greens, beetroot, cheese, walnuts. Whisk oil, vinegar, honey. Dress salad.

N.V.: Calories: 220, Fat: 16 g, Carbohydrates: 14 g, Protein: 8 g, Sugar: 7 g, Sodium: 250 mg, Potassium: 350 mg, Cholesterol: 13 mg.

CURRIED CHICKEN SALAD WITH GRAPES

PREP.T.: 20 min **C. T.:** 0 min **MODE OF COOKING:** Mixing - **SERVINGS:** 4

INGREDIENTS: Cooked chicken breast, 1 cup diced; Grapes, 1 cup halved; Celery, 1/2 cup diced; Greek yogurt, 1/2 cup; Curry powder, 1 tsp; Almonds, 1/4 cup sliced; Salt and pepper to taste.

DIRECTIONS: Combine chicken, grapes, celery. Mix yogurt, curry powder. Combine all, top with almonds.

N.V.: Calories: 180, Fat: 6 g, Carbohydrates: 14 g, Protein: 18 g, Sugar: 8 g, Sodium: 200 mg, Potassium: 300 mg, Cholesterol: 40 mg.

VEGETARIAN SUSHI BOWL

PREP.T.: 15 min **C. T.:** 0 min **MODE OF COOKING:** Assembling - **SERVINGS:** 4

INGREDIENTS: Cooked sushi rice, 2 cups; Cucumber, 1 cup diced; Avocado, 1 diced; Carrot, 1 cup julienned; Edamame, 1 cup; Seaweed, 1/4 cup chopped; Soy sauce, 2 Tbsp.; Sesame oil, 1 tsp; Sesame seeds, 1 tsp.

DIRECTIONS: In bowls, layer rice, vegetables, edamame, seaweed. Drizzle with soy sauce, sesame oil. Sprinkle sesame seeds.

N.V.: Calories: 300, Fat: 9 g, Carbohydrates: 45 g, Protein: 9 g, Sugar: 3 g, Sodium: 600 mg, Potassium: 400 mg, Cholesterol: 0 mg.

MANGO CHICKEN SALAD WITH LIME DRESSING

PREP.T.: 20 min **C. T.:** 0 min **MODE OF COOKING:** Mixing - **SERVINGS:** 4

INGREDIENTS: Cooked chicken breast, 1 cup diced; Mango, 1 cup diced; Avocado, 1 diced; Mixed greens, 4 cups; Red bell pepper, 1/2 cup sliced; Lime juice, 2 Tbsp.; Olive oil, 2 Tbsp.; Honey, 1 tsp; Salt and pepper to taste.

DIRECTIONS: Toss chicken, mango, avocado, greens, pepper. Whisk lime juice, oil, honey. Dress salad.

N.V.: Calories: 270, Fat: 15 g, Carbohydrates: 20 g, Protein: 17 g, Sugar: 10 g, Sodium: 150 mg, Potassium: 500 mg, Cholesterol: 40 mg.

CHAPTER 5: DINNER

Dinner is more than just a meal; it's a time to unwind, reflect on the day, and nourish your body with foods that heal and delight. In "Dinner," we venture into a world where each dish is a celebration of flavor and health, seamlessly integrating the principles of the Galveston Diet to support your journey towards wellness even as the day winds down. These recipes are crafted with a focus on anti-inflammatory ingredients, balanced nutrients, and the pure joy of eating.

We understand that evenings can be just as hectic as any other part of your day, which is why we've included a variety of recipes that cater to all schedules and skill levels. From quick, comforting meals that can be thrown together in under thirty minutes to more elaborate dishes that turn dinner into an occasion, there's something for every night of the week.

Our goal is to ensure that even the busiest days end with a meal that's satisfying, nourishing, and aligned with your health goals. Whether you're sitting down to a family dinner, enjoying a solo meal, or entertaining friends, these recipes are designed to inspire and impress. With a focus on whole foods, minimal processed ingredients, and rich, natural flavors, dinner becomes not just a meal, but an integral part of your wellness journey. Let's close each day with a celebration of health, happiness, and the healing power of good food.

SALMON WITH CRISPY KALE AND QUINOA

PREP.T.: 15 min **C. T.:** 25 min

MODE OF COOKING: Baking - **SERVINGS:** 4

INGREDIENTS: Salmon fillets, 4 (6 oz each); Kale, 2 cups (torn); Quinoa, 1 cup; Olive oil, 2 Tbsp.; Lemon juice, 2 Tbsp.; Salt and pepper, to taste; Garlic, 1 tsp (minced)

DIRECTIONS: Cook quinoa; Toss kale with half the oil, bake at 375°F (190°C) until crisp; Season salmon, top with garlic, bake; Serve with kale, quinoa, drizzle lemon.

N.V.: Calories: 410, Fat: 18 g, Carbohydrates: 30 g, Protein: 35 g, Sugar: 1 g, Sodium: 75 mg, Potassium: 850 mg, Cholesterol: 85 mg

GRILLED CHICKPEA AND VEGETABLE TACOS

PREP.T.: 20 min **C. T.:** 10 min

MODE OF COOKING: Grilling - **SERVINGS:** 4

INGREDIENTS: Chickpeas, 2 cups; Zucchini, 1 cup (sliced); Red bell pepper, 1 cup (sliced); Corn tortillas, 8; Avocado, 1 (sliced); Lime, 1 (for juice); Cumin, 1 tsp; Salt and pepper, to taste; Cilantro, 1/4 cup (chopped)

DIRECTIONS: Toss chickpeas, vegetables with cumin, oil; Grill until charred; Warm tortillas; Fill with mixture, top with avocado, cilantro, lime juice.

N.V.: Calories: 250, Fat: 8 g, Carbohydrates: 38 g, Protein: 9 g, Sugar: 4 g, Sodium: 300 mg, Potassium: 500 mg, Cholesterol: 0 mg

BEEF AND BROCCOLI STIR-FRY

PREP.T.: 15 min **C. T.:** 10 min

MODE OF COOKING: Stir-frying - **SERVINGS:** 4

INGREDIENTS: Beef strips, 1 lb; Broccoli florets, 2 cups; Soy sauce, 1/4 cup; Garlic, 1 Tbsp. (minced); Ginger, 1 Tbsp. (minced); Sesame oil, 1 Tbsp.; Brown sugar, 2 Tbsp.; Cornstarch, 1 tsp; Water, 1/4 cup

DIRECTIONS: Mix soy sauce, garlic, ginger, sugar, cornstarch, water; Stir-fry beef, add broccoli; Pour sauce, cook until thickened.

N.V.: Calories: 280, Fat: 9 g, Carbohydrates: 18 g, Protein: 34 g, Sugar: 8 g, Sodium: 660 mg, Potassium: 600 mg, Cholesterol: 70 mg

MEDITERRANEAN STUFFED EGGPLANT

PREP.T.: 20 min **C. T.:** 40 min

MODE OF COOKING: Baking - **SERVINGS:** 4

INGREDIENTS: Eggplants, 2 (halved); Quinoa, 1 cup (cooked); Tomatoes, 1 cup (diced); Spinach, 1 cup; Feta cheese, 1/2 cup (crumbled); Olives, 1/4 cup (sliced); Garlic, 1 tsp (minced); Olive oil, 2 Tbsp.; Salt and pepper, to taste

DIRECTIONS: Scoop out eggplant; Sauté flesh, garlic, spinach, tomatoes; Mix with quinoa, olives; Stuff eggplants, top with feta; Bake at 375°F (190°C).

N.V.: Calories: 300, Fat: 15 g, Carbohydrates: 35 g, Protein: 10 g, Sugar: 9 g, Sodium: 320 mg, Potassium: 770 mg, Cholesterol: 25 mg

ROASTED BUTTERNUT SQUASH AND CHICKPEA SALAD

PREP.T.: 15 min **C. T.:** 30 min

MODE OF COOKING: Roasting - **SERVINGS:** 4

INGREDIENTS: Butternut squash, 2 cups (cubed); Chickpeas, 1 cup (drained); Mixed greens, 4 cups; Red onion, 1/4 cup (sliced); Pumpkin seeds, 1/4 cup; Olive oil, 3 Tbsp.; Balsamic vinegar, 2 Tbsp.; Honey, 1 Tbsp.; Salt and pepper, to taste

DIRECTIONS: Roast squash, chickpeas with oil, salt, pepper at 425°F (220°C); Mix greens, onion, seeds; Whisk vinegar, honey; Combine, dress salad.

N.V.: Calories: 280, Fat: 14 g, Carbohydrates: 34 g, Protein: 7 g, Sugar: 9 g, Sodium: 30 mg, Potassium: 670 mg, Cholesterol: 0 mg

LEMON GARLIC TILAPIA

PREP.T.: 10 min **C. T.:** 12 min

MODE OF COOKING: Baking - **SERVINGS:** 4

INGREDIENTS: Tilapia fillets, 4; Lemon juice, 2 Tbsp.; Garlic, 2 tsp (minced); Butter, 2 Tbsp.; Parsley, 1 Tbsp. (chopped); Salt and pepper, to taste

DIRECTIONS: Place tilapia in baking dish; Top with garlic, lemon juice, dots of butter; Season; Bake at 400°F (204°C) until flaky; Garnish with parsley.

N.V.: Calories: 180, Fat: 8 g, Carbohydrates: 1 g, Protein: 25 g, Sugar: 0 g, Sodium: 65 mg, Potassium: 350 mg, Cholesterol: 85 mg

THAI COCONUT CURRY TOFU

PREP.T.: 15 min **C. T.:** 20 min

MODE OF COOKING: Sautéing - **SERVINGS:** 4

INGREDIENTS: Tofu, 14 oz (pressed, cubed); Coconut milk, 1 can; Thai curry paste, 2 Tbsp.; Mixed vegetables, 2 cups (e.g., bell pepper, broccoli); Onion, 1 (sliced); Garlic, 1 tsp (minced); Ginger, 1 Tbsp. (grated); Olive oil, 1 Tbsp.; Salt and pepper, to taste

DIRECTIONS: Sauté onion, garlic, ginger in oil; Add curry paste, cook 1 min; Add coconut milk, vegetables; Simmer until tender; Add tofu, heat through.

N.V.: Calories: 260, Fat: 20 g, Carbohydrates: 10 g, Protein: 12 g, Sugar: 3 g, Sodium: 200 mg, Potassium: 300 mg, Cholesterol: 0 mg

ZUCCHINI NOODLE PESTO PASTA

PREP.T.: 15 min **C. T.:** 0 min

MODE OF COOKING: Spiralizing/Mixing - **SERVINGS:** 4

INGREDIENTS: Zucchini, 4 (spiralized); Cherry tomatoes, 1 cup (halved); Pesto, 1/2 cup; Pine nuts, 1/4 cup (toasted); Parmesan cheese, 1/4 cup (grated); Salt and pepper, to taste

DIRECTIONS: Toss zucchini noodles with pesto; Add tomatoes, pine nuts; Season; Serve topped with Parmesan.

N.V.: Calories: 220, Fat: 18 g, Carbohydrates: 8 g, Protein: 6 g, Sugar: 4 g, Sodium: 380 mg, Potassium: 512 mg, Cholesterol: 4 mg

CAULIFLOWER STEAKS WITH CHIMICHURRI SAUCE

PREP.T.: 10 min **C. T.:** 25 min

MODE OF COOKING: Roasting - **SERVINGS:** 4

INGREDIENTS: Cauliflower, 2 heads (sliced into steaks); Olive oil, 2 Tbsp.; Salt and pepper, to taste; For Chimichurri: Parsley, 1 cup (chopped); Garlic, 2 cloves (minced); Red pepper flakes, 1/2 tsp; Olive oil, 1/3 cup; Vinegar, 2 Tbsp.

DIRECTIONS: Brush cauliflower with oil, season; Roast at 425°F (220°C) until tender; Mix chimichurri ingredients; Serve steaks drizzled with sauce.

N.V.: Calories: 250, Fat: 21 g, Carbohydrates: 10 g, Protein: 4 g, Sugar: 3 g, Sodium: 75 mg, Potassium: 640 mg, Cholesterol: 0 mg

WILD MUSHROOM RISOTTO

PREP.T.: 10 min **C. T.:** 25 min

MODE OF COOKING: Stirring - **SERVINGS:** 4

INGREDIENTS: Arborio rice, 1 cup; Wild mushrooms, 2 cups (sliced); Vegetable broth, 4 cups; Onion, 1/2 cup (finely chopped); Garlic, 1 tsp (minced); White wine, 1/2 cup; Parmesan cheese, 1/2 cup (grated); Olive oil, 2 Tbsp.; Thyme, 1 tsp; Salt and pepper, to taste

DIRECTIONS: Sauté mushrooms, onion, garlic in oil; Add rice, cook 1 min; Add wine, then broth gradually, stirring; Finish with Parmesan, thyme.

N.V.: Calories: 380, Fat: 12 g, Carbohydrates: 54 g, Protein: 12 g, Sugar: 2 g, Sodium: 950 mg, Potassium: 300 mg, Cholesterol: 11 mg

SPICED LENTIL SOUP WITH KALE

PREP.T.: 15 min **C. T.:** 30 min

MODE OF COOKING: Simmering - **SERVINGS:** 4

INGREDIENTS: Lentils, 1 cup; Kale, 2 cups (chopped); Carrot, 1 cup (diced); Celery, 1/2 cup (diced); Onion, 1 (diced); Garlic, 2 cloves (minced); Cumin, 1 tsp; Coriander, 1 tsp; Vegetable broth, 6 cups; Olive oil, 2 Tbsp.; Salt and pepper, to taste; Lemon, 1 (juice)

DIRECTIONS: Sauté onion, carrot, celery, garlic in oil; Add spices; Add lentils, broth; Simmer until lentils are tender; Add kale, cook until wilted; Stir in lemon juice.

N.V.: Calories: 240, Fat: 5 g, Carbohydrates: 38 g, Protein: 14 g, Sugar: 5 g, Sodium: 300 mg, Potassium: 710 mg, Cholesterol: 0 mg

HERB-CRUSTED PORK TENDERLOIN

PREP.T.: 20 min **C. T.:** 25 min

MODE OF COOKING: Roasting - **SERVINGS:** 4

INGREDIENTS: Pork tenderloin, 1 lb; Bread crumbs, 1/2 cup; Parsley, 1/4 cup (chopped); Rosemary, 1 Tbsp. (chopped); Thyme, 1 Tbsp. (chopped); Garlic, 2 cloves (minced); Olive oil, 2 Tbsp.; Dijon mustard, 2 Tbsp.; Salt and pepper, to taste

DIRECTIONS: Coat pork with mustard; Mix breadcrumbs, herbs, garlic; Press onto pork; Roast at 375°F (190°C) until cooked; Rest before slicing.

N.V.: Calories: 310, Fat: 12 g, Carbohydrates: 9 g, Protein: 40 g, Sugar: 0 g, Sodium: 350 mg, Potassium: 650 mg, Cholesterol: 110 mg

PARMESAN CRUSTED CHICKEN WITH ARUGULA SALAD

PREP.T.: 15 min **C. T.:** 20 min

MODE OF COOKING: Baking - **SERVINGS:** 4

INGREDIENTS: Chicken breasts, 4; Grated Parmesan cheese, 1 cup; Panko breadcrumbs, 1/2 cup; Olive oil, 2 Tbsp.; Eggs, 2; Arugula, 4 cups; Lemon juice, 2 Tbsp.; Salt and pepper, to taste

DIRECTIONS: Beat eggs; Mix Parmesan, breadcrumbs, salt, pepper; Dip chicken in egg, then breadcrumb mix; Bake at 400°F (204°C) until golden; Toss arugula with lemon juice, olive oil; Serve with chicken.

N.V.: Calories: 360, Fat: 16 g, Carbohydrates: 12 g, Protein: 42 g, Sugar: 1 g, Sodium: 450 mg, Potassium: 300 mg, Cholesterol: 120 mg

VEGETARIAN EGGPLANT LASAGNA

PREP.T.: 30 min **C. T.:** 45 min

MODE OF COOKING: Baking - **SERVINGS:** 6

INGREDIENTS: Eggplant, 2 (sliced); Ricotta cheese, 1 cup; Spinach, 2 cups; Crushed tomatoes, 2 cups; Mozzarella cheese, 1 cup (shredded); Parmesan cheese, 1/2 cup (grated); Garlic, 1 tsp (minced); Olive oil, 2 Tbsp.; Salt and pepper, to taste; Italian seasoning, 1 tsp

DIRECTIONS: Roast eggplant slices brushed with oil at 425°F (220°C); Layer eggplant, ricotta mixed with spinach, tomatoes, and mozzarella in a baking dish; Top with Parmesan, seasoning; Bake at 375°F (190°C).

N.V.: Calories: 280, Fat: 16 g, Carbohydrates: 20 g, Protein: 18 g, Sugar: 8 g, Sodium: 380 mg, Potassium: 550 mg, Cholesterol: 45 mg

SHRIMP AND AVOCADO TACO SALAD

PREP.T.: 20 min **C. T.:** 10 min

MODE OF COOKING: Sautéing - **SERVINGS:** 4

INGREDIENTS: Shrimp, 1 lb (peeled); Avocado, 2 (diced); Romaine lettuce, 4 cups (chopped); Black beans, 1 cup (rinsed); Corn, 1 cup; Cherry tomatoes, 1 cup (halved); Lime juice, 3 Tbsp.; Olive oil, 2 Tbsp.; Cumin, 1 tsp; Salt and pepper, to taste; Tortilla chips, 1 cup (crushed)

DIRECTIONS: Sauté shrimp in 1 Tbsp. oil, cumin, salt, pepper; Combine lettuce, beans, corn, tomatoes, avocado, shrimp; Dress with lime juice, remaining oil; Garnish with chips.

N.V.: Calories: 350, Fat: 18 g, Carbohydrates: 27 g, Protein: 25 g, Sugar: 4 g, Sodium: 300 mg, Potassium: 750 mg, Cholesterol: 180 mg

STUFFED PORTOBELLO MUSHROOMS WITH QUINOA

PREP.T.: 20 min **C. T.:** 25 min

MODE OF COOKING: Baking - **SERVINGS:** 4

INGREDIENTS: Portobello mushroom caps, 4; Quinoa, 1 cup (cooked); Spinach, 1 cup (chopped); Feta cheese, 1/2 cup (crumbled); Cherry tomatoes, 1/2 cup (halved); Garlic, 1 tsp (minced); Olive oil, 2 Tbsp.; Balsamic vinegar, 1 Tbsp.; Salt and pepper, to taste

DIRECTIONS: Remove mushroom stems, brush with oil, vinegar; Bake caps at 375°F (190°C) for 10 min; Mix quinoa, spinach, tomatoes, feta, garlic, stuff mushrooms; Bake 15 min.

N.V.: Calories: 240, Fat: 10 g, Carbohydrates: 30 g, Protein: 10 g, Sugar: 4 g, Sodium: 320 mg, Potassium: 470 mg, Cholesterol: 25 mg

LEMON HERB ROASTED CHICKEN

PREP.T.: 20 min **C. T.:** 1 hr 20 min

MODE OF COOKING: Roasting - **SERVINGS:** 4

INGREDIENTS: Whole chicken, 4 lb; Lemon, 2 (1 juiced, 1 sliced); Garlic, 4 cloves (minced); Fresh rosemary, 2 Tbsp. (chopped); Fresh thyme, 2 Tbsp. (chopped); Olive oil, 3 Tbsp.; Salt and pepper, to taste

DIRECTIONS: Preheat oven to 425°F (220°C); Mix lemon juice, garlic, herbs, oil; Rub on chicken, season; Place lemon slices inside; Roast until juices run clear.

N.V.: Calories: 410, Fat: 24 g, Carbohydrates: 3 g, Protein: 45 g, Sugar: 0 g, Sodium: 340 mg, Potassium: 370 mg, Cholesterol: 130 mg

BALSAMIC GLAZED SALMON

PREP.T.: 10 min **C. T.:** 15 min

MODE OF COOKING: Baking - **SERVINGS:** 4

INGREDIENTS: Salmon fillets, 4 (6 oz each); Balsamic vinegar, 1/4 cup; Honey, 2 Tbsp.; Garlic, 1 tsp (minced); Olive oil, 1 Tbsp.; Salt and pepper, to taste; Fresh dill, for garnish

DIRECTIONS: Mix vinegar, honey, garlic; Brush salmon with mixture, oil; Season; Bake at 400°F (204°C) until glaze is caramelized; Garnish with dill.

N.V.: Calories: 310, Fat: 14 g, Carbohydrates: 9 g, Protein: 35 g, Sugar: 7 g, Sodium: 200 mg, Potassium: 840 mg, Cholesterol: 90 mg

VEGETABLE AND TOFU STIR-FRY

PREP.T.: 15 min **C. T.:** 10 min

MODE OF COOKING: Stir-frying - **SERVINGS:** 4

INGREDIENTS: Firm tofu, 14 oz (cubed); Broccoli, 2 cups (florets); Carrot, 1 cup (sliced); Bell pepper, 1 cup (sliced); Soy sauce, 1/4 cup; Ginger, 1 Tbsp. (grated); Garlic, 2 tsp (minced); Sesame oil, 2 Tbsp.; Sesame seeds, 1 tsp (for garnish)

DIRECTIONS: Press tofu; Stir-fry vegetables in 1 Tbsp. oil; Remove; Stir-fry tofu; Add vegetables, soy sauce, ginger, garlic; Serve sprinkled with sesame seeds.

N.V.: Calories: 220, Fat: 12 g, Carbohydrates: 14 g, Protein: 16 g, Sugar: 5 g, Sodium: 760 mg, Potassium: 300 mg, Cholesterol: 0 mg

CHAPTER 6: SNACKS AND SIDES TO SATISFY YOUR CRAVINGS

In the rhythm of our daily lives, where meals are often bookmarked by moments of hunger and the search for something to satisfy a craving, the role of snacks and sides becomes undeniably significant. "Snacks and Sides to Satisfy Your Cravings" is a chapter dedicated to those in-between moments, offering a collection of recipes that are not only quick and easy to prepare but also align with the nutritional ethos of the Galveston Diet. Here, we understand that snacking is an integral part of our dietary landscape, and with the right choices, it can bolster our health rather than detract from it.

Crafted with anti-inflammatory ingredients, each recipe is a testament to the idea that snacks and sides can be both delicious and beneficial. From crunchy, oven-baked kale chips to savory, spice-infused nuts, and refreshing, zesty salads, these dishes are designed to be enjoyed at any time of the day. They serve as perfect companions to meals or stand-alone treats that can stave off hunger, fuel your body with nutrients, and satisfy those pesky cravings without guilt.

Whether you're in need of a quick energy boost, a comforting nibble, or a flavorful addition to elevate a meal, this chapter promises to deliver. It champions the concept that every bite we take can be an opportunity to nourish and indulge in the pleasures of eating well. So, let's embrace these moments of snacking and side-dishing with enthusiasm and a keen appetite for health.

CRISPY CHICKPEA AND TURMERIC SNACK

PREP.T.: 10 min **C. T.:** 40 min

MODE OF COOKING: Roasting - **SERVINGS:** 4

INGREDIENTS: Chickpeas, 2 cups (drained); Olive oil, 2 Tbsp.; Turmeric, 1 tsp; Garlic powder, 1/2 tsp; Salt, to taste

DIRECTIONS: Toss chickpeas with olive oil, turmeric, garlic powder, salt; Roast at 400°F (204°C) until crispy.

N.V.: Calories: 210, Fat: 10 g, Carbohydrates: 24 g, Protein: 7 g, Sugar: 4 g, Sodium: 300 mg, Potassium: 290 mg, Cholesterol: 0 mg

AVOCADO AND COTTAGE CHEESE DIP

PREP.T.: 5 min **C. T.:** 0 min

MODE OF COOKING: Blending - **SERVINGS:** 4

INGREDIENTS: Avocado, 1 (ripe); Cottage cheese, 1 cup; Lime juice, 1 Tbsp.; Cilantro, 1/4 cup (chopped); Salt and pepper, to taste

DIRECTIONS: Blend avocado, cottage cheese, lime juice, cilantro until smooth; Season.

N.V.: Calories: 160, Fat: 9 g, Carbohydrates: 8 g, Protein: 9 g, Sugar: 2 g, Sodium: 200 mg, Potassium: 250 mg, Cholesterol: 5 mg

SWEET POTATO CHIPS

PREP.T.: 10 min **C. T.:** 20 min

MODE OF COOKING: Baking - **SERVINGS:** 4

INGREDIENTS: Sweet potatoes, 2 (thinly sliced); Olive oil, 2 Tbsp.; Paprika, 1 tsp; Salt, to taste

DIRECTIONS: Toss sweet potato slices with olive oil, paprika, salt; Bake at 375°F (190°C) until crispy.

N.V.: Calories: 150, Fat: 7 g, Carbohydrates: 20 g, Protein: 2 g, Sugar: 4 g, Sodium: 180 mg, Potassium: 300 mg, Cholesterol: 0 mg

ZUCCHINI AND PARMESAN FRITTERS

PREP.T.: 15 min **C. T.:** 10 min

MODE OF COOKING: Frying - **SERVINGS:** 4

INGREDIENTS: Zucchini, 2 cups (grated); Parmesan cheese, 1/2 cup (grated); Eggs, 2; Flour, 1/4 cup; Salt and pepper, to taste; Olive oil, for frying

DIRECTIONS: Mix zucchini, Parmesan, eggs, flour, salt, pepper; Form patties; Fry in olive oil until golden.

N.V.: Calories: 180, Fat: 12 g, Carbohydrates: 8 g, Protein: 10 g, Sugar: 3 g, Sodium: 320 mg, Potassium: 200 mg, Cholesterol: 110 mg

KALE AND ALMOND PESTO

PREP.T.: 10 min **C. T.:** 0 min

MODE OF COOKING: Blending - **SERVINGS:** 4

INGREDIENTS: Kale, 2 cups (chopped); Almonds, 1/2 cup; Garlic, 1 clove; Parmesan cheese, 1/4 cup (grated); Olive oil, 1/2 cup; Lemon juice, 1 Tbsp.; Salt, to taste

DIRECTIONS: Blend kale, almonds, garlic, Parmesan, lemon juice, salt; Gradually add olive oil until smooth.

N.V.: Calories: 310, Fat: 28 g, Carbohydrates: 8 g, Protein: 7 g, Sugar: 1 g, Sodium: 200 mg, Potassium: 300 mg, Cholesterol: 4 mg

CUCUMBER AND DILL YOGURT SALAD

PREP.T.: 10 min **C. T.:** 0 min

MODE OF COOKING: Mixing - **SERVINGS:** 4

INGREDIENTS: Cucumber, 2 cups (sliced); Greek yogurt, 1 cup; Dill, 1/4 cup (chopped); Garlic, 1 tsp (minced); Lemon juice, 1 Tbsp.; Salt and pepper, to taste

DIRECTIONS: Mix cucumber, yogurt, dill, garlic, lemon juice; Season with salt, pepper.

N.V.: Calories: 70, Fat: 1 g, Carbohydrates: 10 g, Protein: 5 g, Sugar: 5 g, Sodium: 40 mg, Potassium: 200 mg, Cholesterol: 5 mg

ROASTED BRUSSELS SPROUTS WITH BACON

PREP.T.: 10 min **C. T.:** 25 min

MODE OF COOKING: Roasting - **SERVINGS:** 4

INGREDIENTS: Brussels sprouts, 2 cups (halved); Bacon, 4 strips (chopped); Olive oil, 1 Tbsp.; Salt and pepper, to taste

DIRECTIONS: Toss Brussels sprouts with bacon, olive oil, salt, pepper; Roast at 400°F (204°C) until crispy.

N.V.: Calories: 150, Fat: 9 g, Carbohydrates: 10 g, Protein: 8 g, Sugar: 2 g, Sodium: 300 mg, Potassium: 440 mg, Cholesterol: 20 mg

SPICY LIME ROASTED NUTS

PREP.T.: 5 min **C. T.:** 15 min

MODE OF COOKING: Roasting - **SERVINGS:** 4

INGREDIENTS: Mixed nuts, 2 cups; Lime juice, 2 Tbsp.; Olive oil, 1 Tbsp.; Chili powder, 1 tsp; Salt, 1/2 tsp

DIRECTIONS: Toss nuts with lime juice, olive oil, chili powder, and salt; Spread on baking sheet; Roast at 350°F (175°C) until golden.

N.V.: Calories: 320, Fat: 28 g, Carbohydrates: 12 g, Protein: 8 g, Sugar: 2 g, Sodium: 300 mg, Potassium: 350 mg, Cholesterol: 0 mg

GARLIC AND HERB MASHED CAULIFLOWER

PREP.T.: 10 min **C. T.:** 15 min

MODE OF COOKING: Boiling/Mashing - **SERVINGS:** 4

INGREDIENTS: Cauliflower, 1 head (cut into florets); Garlic, 2 cloves (minced); Olive oil, 2 Tbsp.; Fresh thyme, 1 tsp; Salt and pepper, to taste

DIRECTIONS: Boil cauliflower until tender; Drain; Mash with garlic, olive oil, thyme; Season with salt, pepper.

N.V.: Calories: 110, Fat: 7 g, Carbohydrates: 10 g, Protein: 4 g, Sugar: 4 g, Sodium: 60 mg, Potassium: 430 mg, Cholesterol: 0 mg

BAKED PARMESAN TOMATO SLICES

PREP.T.: 5 min **C. T.:** 10 min

MODE OF COOKING: Baking - **SERVINGS:** 4

INGREDIENTS: Tomatoes, 4 (sliced); Parmesan cheese, 1/2 cup (grated); Olive oil, 1 Tbsp.; Basil leaves, 1/4 cup (chopped); Salt and pepper, to taste

DIRECTIONS: Place tomato slices on baking sheet; Top with Parmesan, drizzle with oil; Season; Bake at 375°F (190°C) until cheese is golden.

N.V.: Calories: 100, Fat: 7 g, Carbohydrates: 4 g, Protein: 6 g, Sugar: 2 g, Sodium: 200 mg, Potassium: 210 mg, Cholesterol: 11 mg

CINNAMON ROASTED SWEET POTATOES

PREP.T.: 10 min **C. T.:** 25 min

MODE OF COOKING: Roasting - **SERVINGS:** 4

INGREDIENTS: Sweet potatoes, 2 cups (cubed); Olive oil, 2 Tbsp.; Cinnamon, 1 tsp; Salt, 1/4 tsp

DIRECTIONS: Toss sweet potatoes with olive oil, cinnamon, and salt; Roast at 425°F (220°C) until tender.

N.V.: Calories: 140, Fat: 7 g, Carbohydrates: 20 g, Protein: 2 g, Sugar: 5 g, Sodium: 160 mg, Potassium: 310 mg, Cholesterol: 0 mg

CHILLED CUCUMBER SOUP

PREP.T.: 15 min **C. T.:** 0 min

MODE OF COOKING: Blending/Chilling - **SERVINGS:** 4

INGREDIENTS: Cucumbers, 3 (peeled, seeded); Greek yogurt, 1 cup; Dill, 1/4 cup (chopped); Garlic, 1 clove; Lemon juice, 1 Tbsp.; Salt and pepper, to taste

DIRECTIONS: Blend cucumbers, yogurt, dill, garlic, lemon juice until smooth; Chill; Season before serving.

N.V.: Calories: 70, Fat: 1 g, Carbohydrates: 12 g, Protein: 5 g, Sugar: 6 g, Sodium: 50 mg, Potassium: 360 mg, Cholesterol: 5 mg

QUINOA TABBOULEH

PREP.T.: 15 min **C. T.:** 15 min

MODE OF COOKING: Boiling/Chilling - **SERVINGS:** 4

INGREDIENTS: Quinoa, 1 cup (cooked); Cucumber, 1 cup (diced); Tomatoes, 1 cup (diced); Parsley, 1 cup (chopped); Mint, 1/4 cup (chopped); Lemon juice, 3 Tbsp.; Olive oil, 2 Tbsp.; Salt and pepper, to taste

DIRECTIONS: Combine all ingredients in a bowl; Chill for an hour before serving.

N.V.: Calories: 220, Fat: 10 g, Carbohydrates: 30 g, Protein: 6 g, Sugar: 2 g, Sodium: 10 mg, Potassium: 320 mg, Cholesterol: 0 mg

HUMMUS AND VEGETABLE PLATTER

PREP.T.: 10 min **C. T.:** 0 min

MODE OF COOKING: Assembling - **SERVINGS:** 4

INGREDIENTS: Hummus, 1 cup; Carrot sticks, 1 cup; Celery sticks, 1 cup; Bell pepper strips, 1 cup; Cucumber slices, 1 cup; Olive oil, 1 Tbsp. for drizzle; Paprika, for garnish

DIRECTIONS: Arrange vegetables around a bowl of hummus; Drizzle hummus with olive oil, sprinkle paprika.

N.V.: Calories: 150, Fat: 9 g, Carbohydrates: 13 g, Protein: 5 g, Sugar: 4 g, Sodium: 300 mg, Potassium: 360 mg, Cholesterol: 0 mg

CHEESY KALE CHIPS

PREP.T.: 10 min **C. T.:** 15 min

MODE OF COOKING: Baking - **SERVINGS:** 4

INGREDIENTS: Kale leaves, 4 cups (torn); Olive oil, 1 Tbsp.; Nutritional yeast, 2 Tbsp.; Salt, 1/2 tsp

DIRECTIONS: Toss kale with olive oil, nutritional yeast, salt; Spread on baking sheet; Bake at 300°F (150°C) until crisp.

N.V.: Calories: 80, Fat: 5 g, Carbohydrates: 7 g, Protein: 5 g, Sugar: 0 g, Sodium: 250 mg, Potassium: 330 mg, Cholesterol: 0 mg

ROASTED RED PEPPER HUMMUS

PREP.T.: 10 min **C. T.:** 0 min

MODE OF COOKING: Blending - **SERVINGS:** 4

INGREDIENTS: Chickpeas, 1 can (drained); Roasted red peppers, 1/2 cup (chopped); Tahini, 2 Tbsp.; Lemon juice, 1 Tbsp.; Garlic, 1 clove (minced); Olive oil, 2 Tbsp.; Cumin, 1/2 tsp; Salt, to taste

DIRECTIONS: Blend all ingredients until smooth; Adjust seasoning as needed; Serve chilled with a drizzle of olive oil.

N.V.: Calories: 190, Fat: 10 g, Carbohydrates: 20 g, Protein: 6 g, Sugar: 3 g, Sodium: 300 mg, Potassium: 210 mg, Cholesterol: 0 mg

BAKED SWEET POTATO FRIES

PREP.T.: 15 min **C. T.:** 30 min

MODE OF COOKING: Baking - **SERVINGS:** 4

INGREDIENTS: Sweet potatoes, 3 (peeled, cut into fries); Olive oil, 3 Tbsp.; Paprika, 1 tsp; Garlic powder, 1 tsp; Salt and pepper, to taste

DIRECTIONS: Toss sweet potato fries with olive oil, paprika, garlic powder, salt, and pepper; Bake at 425°F (220°C) until crispy.

N.V.: Calories: 200, Fat: 9 g, Carbohydrates: 28 g, Protein: 2 g, Sugar: 6 g, Sodium: 200 mg, Potassium: 475 mg, Cholesterol: 0 mg

PEANUT BUTTER ENERGY BALLS

PREP.T.: 15 min **C. T.:** 0 min

MODE OF COOKING: Mixing - **SERVINGS:** 4

INGREDIENTS: Oats, 1 cup; Peanut butter, 1/2 cup; Honey, 1/4 cup; Chia seeds, 2 Tbsp.; Flaxseed, 2 Tbsp. (ground); Chocolate chips, 1/4 cup

DIRECTIONS: Mix all ingredients; Form into balls; Chill in the refrigerator until firm.

N.V.: Calories: 250, Fat: 14 g, Carbohydrates: 28 g, Protein: 7 g, Sugar: 12 g, Sodium: 75 mg, Potassium: 200 mg, Cholesterol: 0 mg

CREAMY AVOCADO DIP

PREP.T.: 10 min **C. T.:** 0 min

MODE OF COOKING: Blending - **SERVINGS:** 4

INGREDIENTS: Avocados, 2; Greek yogurt, 1/2 cup; Lime juice, 2 Tbsp.; Cilantro, 1/4 cup; Garlic, 1 clove; Salt and pepper, to taste

DIRECTIONS: Blend avocados, yogurt, lime juice, cilantro, garlic until smooth; Season with salt, pepper.

N.V.: Calories: 220, Fat: 17 g, Carbohydrates: 14 g, Protein: 5 g, Sugar: 2 g, Sodium: 60 mg, Potassium: 560 mg, Cholesterol: 2 mg

SPICY PUMPKIN SEEDS

PREP.T.: 5 min **C. T.:** 20 min

MODE OF COOKING: Roasting - **SERVINGS:** 4

INGREDIENTS: Pumpkin seeds, 1 cup (cleaned); Olive oil, 1 Tbsp.; Chili powder, 1 tsp; Cumin, 1/2 tsp; Salt, to taste

DIRECTIONS: Toss pumpkin seeds with olive oil, chili powder, cumin, and salt; Roast at 300°F (150°C) until golden and crunchy.

N.V.: Calories: 180, Fat: 15 g, Carbohydrates: 3 g, Protein: 9 g, Sugar: 0 g, Sodium: 150 mg, Potassium: 129 mg, Cholesterol: 0 mg

CHAPTER 7: SWEET TREATS FOR GUILT-FREE INDULGENCE

In the journey towards wellness and balanced eating, indulging in sweet treats doesn't have to be a source of guilt. "Sweet Treats for Guilt-Free Indulgence" is a chapter dedicated to reimagining dessert in a way that aligns with the principles of the Galveston Diet, ensuring that every bite not only satisfies your sweet tooth but also nourishes your body. Here, we embrace the joy of dessert, crafting recipes that incorporate wholesome ingredients, natural sweeteners, and the power of anti-inflammatory foods.

This chapter is designed to debunk the myth that healthy eating means sacrificing the foods you love. Instead, we offer a collection of desserts that are as beneficial as they are delicious, from decadent chocolate treats rich in antioxidants to fruity delights bursting with vitamins and fiber. Each recipe is a testament to the idea that dessert can be a harmonious part of a healthful diet, contributing to your wellness journey rather than detracting from it.

Whether you're looking for a simple, no-bake option for busy nights, a refined sugar-free solution to your cravings, or a show-stopping finale for a special meal, these recipes promise satisfaction without compromise. They're about celebrating natural flavors, experimenting with nutritious ingredients, and finding pleasure in the act of creation and consumption.

Let's embark on a journey of guilt-free indulgence, where the end of the meal is just the beginning of experiencing the joy and abundance that comes with eating well.

BLACKBERRY BALSAMIC BLISS BITES

PREP.T.: 10 min **C. T.:** 0 min

MODE OF COOKING: Chilling - **SERVINGS:** 4

INGREDIENTS: Blackberries 1 cup; Greek yogurt 1/2 cup; Balsamic vinegar 1 Tbsp.; Honey 1 Tbsp.; Crushed almonds 1/4 cup; Fresh mint leaves for garnish

DIRECTIONS: Dip blackberries in Greek yogurt, then drizzle with a mixture of balsamic vinegar and honey. Roll in crushed almonds, garnish with mint, and chill.

N.V.: Calories: 120, Fat: 4 g, Carbohydrates: 18 g, Protein: 4 g, Sugar: 15 g, Sodium: 20 mg, Potassium: 150 mg, Cholesterol: 5 mg

---

CINNAMON SPICED BAKED PEARS

PREP.T.: 5 min **C. T.:** 25 min

MODE OF COOKING: Baking - **SERVINGS:** 4

INGREDIENTS: Pears 4 (halved and cored); Honey 2 Tbsp.; Cinnamon 1 tsp; Nutmeg 1/4 tsp; Walnuts 1/4 cup (chopped); Ricotta cheese 1/2 cup

DIRECTIONS: Arrange pear halves on baking sheet. Drizzle with honey, sprinkle with cinnamon, nutmeg; bake. Serve with walnuts, dollop of ricotta.

N.V.: Calories: 150, Fat: 5 g, Carbohydrates: 27 g, Protein: 3 g, Sugar: 20 g, Sodium: 25 mg, Potassium: 200 mg, Cholesterol: 10 mg

---

LEMON RICOTTA BERRY PARFAIT

PREP.T.: 10 min **C. T.:** 0 min

MODE OF COOKING: Layering - **SERVINGS:** 4

INGREDIENTS: Ricotta cheese 1 cup; Lemon zest 1 tsp; Honey 2 Tbsp.; Mixed berries 2 cups; Granola 1/2 cup

DIRECTIONS: Mix ricotta with lemon zest, layer with berries and granola in glasses. Drizzle with honey.

N.V.: Calories: 180, Fat: 8 g, Carbohydrates: 22 g, Protein: 8 g, Sugar: 14 g, Sodium: 85 mg, Potassium: 210 mg, Cholesterol: 30 mg

---

GINGER PEAR SORBET

PREP.T.: 10 min **C. T.:** 0 min (plus freezing)

MODE OF COOKING: Freezing - **SERVINGS:** 4

INGREDIENTS: Pears 3 (ripe, peeled and chopped); Lemon juice 1 Tbsp.; Honey 2 Tbsp.; Fresh ginger 1 tsp (grated); Water 1/2 cup

DIRECTIONS: Puree pears, lemon juice, honey, ginger, and water until smooth. Freeze until firm. Serve chilled.

N.V.: Calories: 100, Fat: 0 g, Carbohydrates: 27 g, Protein: 1 g, Sugar: 22 g, Sodium: 2 mg, Potassium: 190 mg, Cholesterol: 0 mg

COCONUT DUSTED CHOCOLATE FIGS

PREP.T.: 15 min **C. T.:** 0 min

MODE OF COOKING: Chilling - **SERVINGS:** 4

INGREDIENTS: Figs 8; Dark chocolate 1/2 cup (melted); Coconut flakes 1/4 cup; Almonds 1/4 cup (chopped)

DIRECTIONS: Dip figs in melted chocolate, roll in coconut flakes and almonds. Chill until set.

N.V.: Calories: 200, Fat: 10 g, Carbohydrates: 28 g, Protein: 3 g, Sugar: 24 g, Sodium: 20 mg, Potassium: 300 mg, Cholesterol: 0 mg

ALMOND JOY ENERGY BALLS

PREP.T.: 20 min **C. T.:** 0 min

MODE OF COOKING: Mixing - **SERVINGS:** 4

INGREDIENTS: Dates 1 cup (pitted); Almonds 1/2 cup; Unsweetened coconut flakes 1/2 cup; Cocoa powder 2 Tbsp.; Vanilla extract 1 tsp; Sea salt a pinch

DIRECTIONS: Process dates, almonds, coconut, cocoa, vanilla, salt until sticky. Roll into balls, chill.

N.V.: Calories: 150, Fat: 8 g, Carbohydrates: 18 g, Protein: 3 g, Sugar: 14 g, Sodium: 75 mg, Potassium: 210 mg, Cholesterol: 0 mg

MAPLE CINNAMON ROASTED ALMONDS

PREP.T.: 5 min **C. T.:** 15 min

MODE OF COOKING: Roasting - **SERVINGS:** 4

INGREDIENTS: Almonds 1 cup; Maple syrup 2 Tbsp.; Cinnamon 1 tsp; Sea salt a pinch

DIRECTIONS: Toss almonds with maple syrup, cinnamon, salt. Roast at 350°F (175°C) until fragrant.

N.V.: Calories: 220, Fat: 18 g, Carbohydrates: 14 g, Protein: 6 g, Sugar: 8 g, Sodium: 60 mg, Potassium: 260 mg, Cholesterol: 0 mg

HONEY-LIME YOGURT FRUIT SALAD

PREP.T.: 10 min **C. T.:** 0 min

MODE OF COOKING: Mixing - **SERVINGS:** 4

INGREDIENTS: Mixed berries 2 cups; Kiwi 2 (sliced); Grapes 1 cup; Greek yogurt 1 cup; Honey 2 Tbsp.; Lime zest 1 tsp; Lime juice 1 Tbsp.

DIRECTIONS: Combine fruit in a bowl. Mix yogurt, honey, lime zest, and juice separately, then pour over fruit and gently toss.

N.V.: Calories: 150, Fat: 1 g, Carbohydrates: 34 g, Protein: 5 g, Sugar: 28 g, Sodium: 15 mg, Potassium: 320 mg, Cholesterol: 3 mg

PISTACHIO-CRUSTED CHOCOLATE DATES

PREP.T.: 15 min **C. T.:** 0 min

MODE OF COOKING: Chilling - **SERVINGS:** 4

INGREDIENTS: Dates 12; Dark chocolate 1/2 cup (melted); Pistachios 1/2 cup (finely chopped); Sea salt a pinch

DIRECTIONS: Pit dates, dip in melted chocolate, roll in pistachios, sprinkle with sea salt, and chill until set.

N.V.: Calories: 210, Fat: 9 g, Carbohydrates: 31 g, Protein: 4 g, Sugar: 26 g, Sodium: 25 mg, Potassium: 300 mg, Cholesterol: 0 mg

VANILLA BEAN AND BERRY POPSICLES

PREP.T.: 15 min (plus freezing time) **C. T.:** 0 min

MODE OF COOKING: Freezing - **SERVINGS:** 4

INGREDIENTS: Greek yogurt 1 cup; Mixed berries 1 cup; Honey 2 Tbsp.; Vanilla bean 1 (seeds scraped); Water 1/4 cup

DIRECTIONS: Blend yogurt, berries, honey, vanilla seeds, and water until smooth. Pour into popsicle molds and freeze.

N.V.: Calories: 120, Fat: 1 g, Carbohydrates: 24 g, Protein: 5 g, Sugar: 20 g, Sodium: 30 mg, Potassium: 180 mg, Cholesterol: 5 mg

CACAO NIB AND SEA SALT DARK CHOCOLATE BARK

PREP.T.: 10 min **C. T.:** 0 min (plus chilling)

MODE OF COOKING: Chilling - **SERVINGS:** 4

INGREDIENTS: Dark chocolate 1 cup (melted); Cacao nibs 1/4 cup; Sea salt flakes 1 tsp

DIRECTIONS: Spread melted chocolate on a baking sheet, sprinkle with cacao nibs and sea salt, chill until set, break into pieces.

N.V.: Calories: 200, Fat: 14 g, Carbohydrates: 18 g, Protein: 2 g, Sugar: 12 g, Sodium: 230 mg, Potassium: 220 mg, Cholesterol: 0 mg

ZESTY LEMON SQUARES

PREP.T.: 20 min **C. T.:** 25 min

MODE OF COOKING: Baking - **SERVINGS:** 4

INGREDIENTS: Almond flour 1 cup; Butter 1/4 cup (melted); Honey 1/4 cup; Lemons 2 (juice and zest); Eggs 2; Coconut flour 1 Tbsp.

DIRECTIONS: Mix almond flour with butter, press into pan for crust; blend eggs, lemon, honey for filling, pour over crust, bake at 350°F (175°C).

N.V.: Calories: 320, Fat: 22 g, Carbohydrates: 24 g, Protein: 8 g, Sugar: 18 g, Sodium: 60 mg, Potassium: 100 mg, Cholesterol: 110 mg

SPICED ROASTED CHICKPEAS

PREP.T.: 10 min **C. T.:** 30 min

MODE OF COOKING: Roasting - **SERVINGS:** 4

INGREDIENTS: Chickpeas 2 cups (drained and dried); Olive oil 1 Tbsp.; Cinnamon 1 tsp; Nutmeg 1/2 tsp; Honey 2 Tbsp.; Salt a pinch

DIRECTIONS: Toss chickpeas with oil, cinnamon, nutmeg, and honey; roast at 400°F (204°C) until crispy.

N.V.: Calories: 180, Fat: 5 g, Carbohydrates: 30 g, Protein: 6 g, Sugar: 11 g, Sodium: 300 mg, Potassium: 330 mg, Cholesterol: 0 mg

MATCHA GREEN TEA TRUFFLES

PREP.T.: 20 min **C. T.:** 0 min (plus chilling)

MODE OF COOKING: Chilling - **SERVINGS:** 4

INGREDIENTS: White chocolate 1 cup (melted); Heavy cream 1/4 cup; Matcha powder 2 Tbsp. (plus extra for dusting); Butter 1 Tbsp.

DIRECTIONS: Mix melted chocolate, cream, matcha, and butter until smooth, chill until firm, roll into balls, dust with matcha.

N.V.: Calories: 310, Fat: 22 g, Carbohydrates: 25 g, Protein: 3 g, Sugar: 22 g, Sodium: 50 mg, Potassium: 110 mg, Cholesterol: 35 mg

CHAPTER 8: BEVERAGES TO HYDRATE AND REFRESH

In the harmonious journey of nourishing our bodies and souls, the significance of hydration cannot be overstated. Yet, in our quest for optimal health and wellness, the beverages we choose to sip on throughout the day hold power far beyond mere hydration. This is the heart of Chapter 8: a celebration of drinks that do more than quench thirst—they rejuvenate, heal, and invigorate.

Here, we venture into the art of crafting beverages that not only hydrate but also refresh the spirit and enhance our overall well-being. From the invigorating morning sip that awakens the senses to the soothing evening concoction that eases the soul into tranquility, each recipe is imbued with ingredients purposefully chosen for their healthful benefits and anti-inflammatory properties.

Imagine the zest of citrus fruits infusing your water with not just flavor but also a bounty of vitamin C, or the calming allure of a lavender-infused tea that promises a serene end to a bustling day. We explore the ancient roots of herbal tonics revered for their healing properties, bringing age-old wisdom into the simplicity of your glass.

In a world where the choices of what to drink are endless and often overwhelming, this chapter serves as your compass, guiding you towards beverages that nourish as much as they delight. It's an invitation to transform the mundane act of hydration into a mindful ritual, where each sip is a step towards a more vibrant and healthful existence. Let's raise our glasses to the joy of drinking wisely and well, infusing every day with flavors that refresh, restore, and inspire.

GREEN TEA LIME MINT REFRESHER

PREP.T.: 5 min **C. T.:** 0 min

MODE OF COOKING: Mixing - **SERVINGS:** 2

INGREDIENTS: Green tea bags 2; Water 2 cups (hot); Lime 1 (juiced); Mint leaves 10; Honey 1 Tbsp.; Ice cubes as needed

DIRECTIONS: Steep tea bags in hot water for 3-5 min; Remove bags; Cool tea; Mix in lime juice, mint, honey; Serve over ice.

N.V.: Calories: 40, Fat: 0 g, Carbohydrates: 10 g, Protein: 0 g, Sugar: 9 g, Sodium: 5 mg, Potassium: 25 mg, Cholesterol: 0 mg

CUCUMBER LEMON DETOX WATER

PREP.T.: 10 min **C. T.:** 0 min

MODE OF COOKING: Infusing - **SERVINGS:** 4

INGREDIENTS: Cucumber 1 (sliced); Lemon 1 (sliced); Water 1 quart; Ice cubes as needed; Mint leaves 10 (optional)

DIRECTIONS: Combine cucumber, lemon slices, and mint in a pitcher; Fill with water; Chill for 1 hr; Serve over ice.

N.V.: Calories: 5, Fat: 0 g, Carbohydrates: 1 g, Protein: 0 g, Sugar: 0 g, Sodium: 0 mg, Potassium: 34 mg, Cholesterol: 0 mg

TURMERIC GINGER TEA

PREP.T.: 5 min **C. T.:** 10 min

MODE OF COOKING: Simmering - **SERVINGS:** 2

INGREDIENTS: Water 2 cups; Turmeric powder 1 tsp; Ginger 1 inch (sliced); Honey 1 Tbsp.; Lemon juice 1 tsp

DIRECTIONS: Boil water with turmeric and ginger; Simmer for 10 min; Strain; Stir in honey and lemon juice; Serve hot.

N.V.: Calories: 25, Fat: 0 g, Carbohydrates: 6 g, Protein: 0 g, Sugar: 6 g, Sodium: 1 mg, Potassium: 10 mg, Cholesterol: 0 mg

BEETROOT AND BERRY SMOOTHIE

PREP.T.: 5 min **C. T.:** 0 min

MODE OF COOKING: Blending - **SERVINGS:** 2

INGREDIENTS: Beetroot 1 (cooked and peeled); Mixed berries 1 cup; Banana 1; Almond milk 1 cup; Honey 1 Tbsp.

DIRECTIONS: Blend all ingredients until smooth; Add ice to preference; Serve immediately.

N.V.: Calories: 150, Fat: 1 g, Carbohydrates: 36 g, Protein: 2 g, Sugar: 28 g, Sodium: 55 mg, Potassium: 400 mg, Cholesterol: 0 mg

CARROT GINGER JUICE

PREP.T.: 10 min **C. T.:** 0 min

MODE OF COOKING: Juicing - **SERVINGS:** 2

INGREDIENTS: Carrots 4 (peeled); Ginger 1 inch; Lemon 1/2 (juiced); Water 1 cup; Ice cubes as needed

DIRECTIONS: Juice carrots and ginger; Mix in lemon juice and water; Serve over ice.

N.V.: Calories: 70, Fat: 0.5 g, Carbohydrates: 16 g, Protein: 1 g, Sugar: 6 g, Sodium: 70 mg, Potassium: 450 mg, Cholesterol: 0 mg

SPARKLING MINT LIMEADE

PREP.T.: 10 min **C. T.:** 0 min

MODE OF COOKING: Mixing - **SERVINGS:** 4

INGREDIENTS: Lime juice 1/2 cup; Honey 1/4 cup; Mint leaves 20; Sparkling water 4 cups; Ice cubes as needed

DIRECTIONS: Dissolve honey in lime juice; Add mint; Muddle lightly; Mix with sparkling water; Serve over ice.

N.V.: Calories: 60, Fat: 0 g, Carbohydrates: 16 g, Protein: 0 g, Sugar: 15 g, Sodium: 10 mg, Potassium: 20 mg, Cholesterol: 0 mg

WATERMELON COCONUT HYDRATOR

PREP.T.: 10 min **C. T.:** 0 min

MODE OF COOKING: Blending - **SERVINGS:** 2

INGREDIENTS: Watermelon 2 cups (cubed); Coconut water 1 cup; Lime juice 1 Tbsp.; Mint leaves 5; Ice cubes as needed

DIRECTIONS: Blend watermelon, coconut water, and lime; Stir in mint leaves; Serve over ice.

N.V.: Calories: 80, Fat: 0.5 g, Carbohydrates: 19 g, Protein: 1 g, Sugar: 15 g, Sodium: 25 mg, Potassium: 300 mg, Cholesterol: 0 mg

ALMOND MILK CHAI LATTE

PREP.T.: 5 min **C. T.:** 10 min

MODE OF COOKING: Simmering - **SERVINGS:** 2

INGREDIENTS: Almond milk 2 cups; Black tea bags 2; Cinnamon stick 1; Cardamom pods 4 (crushed); Cloves 4; Honey 1 Tbsp.

DIRECTIONS: Simmer almond milk with spices, tea bags; Remove tea and spices; Stir in honey; Serve hot.

N.V.: Calories: 90, Fat: 3 g, Carbohydrates: 14 g, Protein: 1 g, Sugar: 12 g, Sodium: 80 mg, Potassium: 50 mg, Cholesterol: 0 mg

PEACH GINGER ICED TEA

PREP.T.: 10 min **C. T.:** 5 min (plus chilling)

MODE OF COOKING: Simmering - **SERVINGS:** 4

INGREDIENTS: Black tea bags 4; Water 4 cups; Peach 1 (sliced); Ginger 1 inch (sliced); Honey 2 Tbsp.; Ice cubes as needed

DIRECTIONS: Boil water with ginger; Remove from heat, add tea bags, steep for 5 min; Remove tea bags and ginger; Add honey, stir until dissolved; Chill; Serve over ice with peach slices.

N.V.: Calories: 50, Fat: 0 g, Carbohydrates: 13 g, Protein: 0 g, Sugar: 12 g, Sodium: 10 mg, Potassium: 30 mg, Cholesterol: 0 mg

KIWI CUCUMBER AGUA FRESCA

PREP.T.: 10 min **C. T.:** 0 min

MODE OF COOKING: Blending - **SERVINGS:** 4

INGREDIENTS: Kiwi 4 (peeled); Cucumber 1 (peeled, seeded); Lime juice 1/4 cup; Water 3 cups; Honey 1 Tbsp.; Ice cubes as needed

DIRECTIONS: Blend kiwi, cucumber, lime juice, and water until smooth; Strain if desired; Stir in honey; Serve over ice.

N.V.: Calories: 60, Fat: 0.5 g, Carbohydrates: 14 g, Protein: 1 g, Sugar: 11 g, Sodium: 5 mg, Potassium: 250 mg, Cholesterol: 0 mg

BLUEBERRY LAVENDER LEMONADE

PREP.T.: 15 min **C. T.:** 5 min (plus chilling)

MODE OF COOKING: Boiling - **SERVINGS:** 4

INGREDIENTS: Blueberries 1 cup; Water 4 cups; Lemon juice 1/2 cup; Lavender flowers 1 Tbsp. (edible); Honey 3 Tbsp.; Ice cubes as needed

DIRECTIONS: Boil 1 cup water with lavender, let steep for 5 min; Strain; Blend lavender water with blueberries, strain; Mix in remaining water, lemon juice, honey; Chill; Serve over ice.

N.V.: Calories: 80, Fat: 0 g, Carbohydrates: 21 g, Protein: 0 g, Sugar: 18 g, Sodium: 5 mg, Potassium: 40 mg, Cholesterol: 0 mg

MANGO PINEAPPLE SMOOTHIE

PREP.T.: 5 min **C. T.:** 0 min

MODE OF COOKING: Blending - **SERVINGS:** 2

INGREDIENTS: Mango 1 (peeled, cubed); Pineapple 1 cup (cubed); Coconut water 1 cup; Ice cubes as needed; Honey 1 tsp (optional)

DIRECTIONS: Blend mango, pineapple, coconut water, and ice until smooth; Add honey if desired; Serve immediately.

N.V.: Calories: 120, Fat: 0.5 g, Carbohydrates: 30 g, Protein: 1 g, Sugar: 28 g, Sodium: 30 mg, Potassium: 400 mg, Cholesterol: 0 mg

STRAWBERRY BASIL KOMBUCHA

PREP.T.: 10 min **C. T.:** 0 min

MODE OF COOKING: Mixing - **SERVINGS:** 4

INGREDIENTS: Kombucha 4 cups (plain); Strawberries 1 cup (sliced); Basil leaves 10; Ice cubes as needed

DIRECTIONS: Divide strawberries and basil among glasses; Muddle lightly; Pour kombucha over; Serve with ice.

N.V.: Calories: 30, Fat: 0 g, Carbohydrates: 7 g, Protein: 0 g, Sugar: 6 g, Sodium: 10 mg, Potassium: 50 mg, Cholesterol: 0 mg

RASPBERRY PEACH ICED TEA

PREP.T.: 10 min **C. T.:** 5 min (plus chilling)

MODE OF COOKING: Steeping - **SERVINGS:** 4

INGREDIENTS: Black tea bags 4; Water 4 cups (hot); Raspberries 1 cup; Peach 1 (sliced); Honey 2 Tbsp.; Ice cubes as needed

DIRECTIONS: Steep tea bags in hot water for 5 min; Remove tea bags; Cool; Muddle raspberries and peach slices in a pitcher; Add cooled tea, honey; Stir well; Chill; Serve over ice.

N.V.: Calories: 50, Fat: 0 g, Carbohydrates: 13 g, Protein: 0 g, Sugar: 12 g, Sodium: 10 mg, Potassium: 30 mg, Cholesterol: 0 mg

POMEGRANATE MINT SPARKLER

PREP.T.: 10 min **C. T.:** 0 min

MODE OF COOKING: Mixing - **SERVINGS:** 4

INGREDIENTS: Pomegranate juice 2 cups; Sparkling water 2 cups; Mint leaves 12; Lime 2 (juiced); Honey 1 Tbsp.; Pomegranate seeds for garnish; Ice cubes as needed

DIRECTIONS: In a pitcher, mix pomegranate juice, lime juice, honey; Add sparkling water; Garnish with mint leaves, pomegranate seeds; Serve over ice.

N.V.: Calories: 70, Fat: 0 g, Carbohydrates: 18 g, Protein: 0 g, Sugar: 17 g, Sodium: 25 mg, Potassium: 150 mg, Cholesterol: 0 mg

CHILLED CUCUMBER AVOCADO SOUP

PREP.T.: 15 min **C. T.:** 0 min

MODE OF COOKING: Blending - **SERVINGS:** 4

INGREDIENTS: Cucumber 2 (peeled, seeded); Avocado 1; Yogurt 1 cup (plain); Lime juice 1 Tbsp.; Garlic 1 clove; Salt and pepper to taste; Water 1 cup; Dill 1 Tbsp. (chopped)

DIRECTIONS: Blend all ingredients until smooth; Chill for at least 1 hr; Serve cold garnished with dill.

N.V.: Calories: 150, Fat: 10 g, Carbohydrates: 12 g, Protein: 4 g, Sugar: 6 g, Sodium: 60 mg, Potassium: 450 mg, Cholesterol: 5 mg

CHAPTER 9: FISH AND SEAFOOD

Embarking on a journey through the world of fish and seafood is akin to diving into a vast ocean of flavors, textures, and health benefits that are as deep and varied as the sea itself. In this chapter, we'll navigate the vibrant waters of piscatorial delights, offering you a treasure trove of recipes that not only tantalize your taste buds but also bolster your health, aligning perfectly with the Galveston Diet's focus on anti-inflammatory and hormone-balancing foods.

The ocean provides us with an abundance of gifts, from the lean, protein-packed offerings of wild-caught salmon, rich in Omega-3 fatty acids that combat inflammation and support brain health, to the delicate, iodine-rich profiles of shellfish, which play a crucial role in thyroid health and metabolic balance. We'll explore how to select the freshest catches, the importance of sustainability, and how to incorporate a variety of fish and seafood into your diet in ways that are both simple and sophisticated.

But it's not just about the ingredients; it's about the journey. Each recipe in this chapter is crafted to bring joy and ease to your kitchen, turning the sometimes-intimidating task of cooking fish into a confident, creative, and delicious endeavor. Whether you're a seasoned seafood chef or new to the maritime flavors, you'll find dishes here that will make the heart of your kitchen beat with the pulse of the ocean's tide, inviting you into a world where every meal is an opportunity to nourish your body, delight your senses, and pay homage to the incredible resources our oceans offer. Let's set sail together into the flavorful horizon of fish and seafood, where each dish is a step closer to vibrant health and wellness.

LEMON-HERB GRILLED SALMON

PREP.T.: 10 min **C. T.:** 15 min
MODE OF COOKING: Grilling - **SERVINGS:** 4
INGREDIENTS: Salmon fillets 4 (6 oz each); Olive oil 2 Tbsp.; Lemon 1 (juiced); Garlic 2 cloves (minced); Dill 1 Tbsp.; Salt and pepper to taste
DIRECTIONS: Marinate salmon with lemon juice, garlic, dill, oil, salt, and pepper; Grill over medium heat until flaky.

N.V.: Calories: 280, Fat: 15 g, Carbohydrates: 1 g, Protein: 34 g, Sugar: 0 g, Sodium: 75 mg, Potassium: 830 mg, Cholesterol: 85 mg

SHRIMP AND AVOCADO TACOS

PREP.T.: 15 min **C. T.:** 5 min

MODE OF COOKING: Sautéing - **SERVINGS:** 4

INGREDIENTS: Shrimp peeled 1 lb; Avocados 2 (sliced); Cabbage 2 cups (shredded); Lime 2 (juiced); Cilantro 1/4 cup (chopped); Corn tortillas 8; Salt and pepper to taste

DIRECTIONS: Sauté shrimp with lime juice, salt, and pepper; Assemble tacos with shrimp, avocado, cabbage, cilantro in tortillas.

N.V.: Calories: 300, Fat: 12 g, Carbohydrates: 28 g, Protein: 25 g, Sugar: 2 g, Sodium: 300 mg, Potassium: 600 mg, Cholesterol: 180 mg

BAKED COD WITH CRISPY PARMESAN CRUST

PREP.T.: 10 min **C. T.:** 20 min

MODE OF COOKING: Baking - **SERVINGS:** 4

INGREDIENTS: Cod fillets 4 (6 oz each); Parmesan cheese 1/2 cup (grated); Panko breadcrumbs 1/2 cup; Olive oil 2 Tbsp.; Paprika 1 tsp; Salt and pepper to taste

DIRECTIONS: Mix Parmesan, panko, paprika, salt, pepper; Coat cod in oil, then breadcrumb mix; Bake at 400°F (204°C).

N.V.: Calories: 220, Fat: 8 g, Carbohydrates: 9 g, Protein: 30 g, Sugar: 1 g, Sodium: 390 mg, Potassium: 460 mg, Cholesterol: 60 mg

GARLIC LEMON SCALLOPS

PREP.T.: 5 min **C. T.:** 10 min

MODE OF COOKING: Sautéing - **SERVINGS:** 4

INGREDIENTS: Scallops 1 lb; Butter 2 Tbsp.; Garlic 3 cloves (minced); Lemon 1 (juiced); Parsley 2 Tbsp. (chopped); Salt and pepper to taste

DIRECTIONS: Sauté garlic in butter; Add scallops, cook until golden; Finish with lemon juice, parsley.

N.V.: Calories: 200, Fat: 8 g, Carbohydrates: 5 g, Protein: 27 g, Sugar: 0 g, Sodium: 540 mg, Potassium: 380 mg, Cholesterol: 56 mg

SPICY TUNA STUFFED AVOCADOS

PREP.T.: 10 min **C. T.:** 0 min

MODE OF COOKING: Mixing - **SERVINGS:** 4

INGREDIENTS: Avocados 4; Canned tuna 2 cups (drained); Mayonnaise 1/4 cup; Sriracha 2 Tbsp.; Lime 1 (juiced); Cilantro 1/4 cup (chopped); Salt to taste

DIRECTIONS: Mix tuna, mayonnaise, sriracha, lime juice, cilantro, salt; Stuff into halved avocados.

N.V.: Calories: 320, Fat: 24 g, Carbohydrates: 10 g, Protein: 20 g, Sugar: 2 g, Sodium: 320 mg, Potassium: 850 mg, Cholesterol: 30 mg

MEDITERRANEAN SEA BASS EN PAPILLOTE

PREP.T.: 15 min **C. T.:** 20 min

MODE OF COOKING: Baking - **SERVINGS:** 4

INGREDIENTS: Sea bass fillets 4; Cherry tomatoes 1 cup; Olives 1/2 cup; Capers 1 Tbsp.; Lemon slices 8; Olive oil 2 Tbsp.; Salt and pepper to taste

DIRECTIONS: Place each fillet on parchment with tomatoes, olives, capers, lemon; Drizzle with oil, season; Fold parchment, bake at 375°F (190°C).

N.V.: Calories: 230, Fat: 10 g, Carbohydrates: 4 g, Protein: 30 g, Sugar: 1 g, Sodium: 300 mg, Potassium: 600 mg, Cholesterol: 80 mg

HONEY GLAZED SALMON WITH GINGER

PREP.T.: 10 min **C. T.:** 15 min

MODE OF COOKING: Broiling - **SERVINGS:** 4

INGREDIENTS: Salmon fillets 4; Honey 3 Tbsp.; Soy sauce 2 Tbsp.; Ginger 1 Tbsp. (grated); Garlic 1 tsp (minced); Sesame seeds 1 tsp

DIRECTIONS: Whisk honey, soy sauce, ginger, garlic; Brush on salmon; Broil until caramelized; Sprinkle with sesame seeds.

N.V.: Calories: 310, Fat: 14 g, Carbohydrates: 15 g, Protein: 35 g, Sugar: 12 g, Sodium: 480 mg, Potassium: 840 mg, Cholesterol: 90 mg

CAJUN SHRIMP AND QUINOA BOWL

PREP.T.: 15 min **C. T.:** 20 min

MODE OF COOKING: Sautéing - **SERVINGS:** 4

INGREDIENTS: Shrimp 1 lb (peeled); Quinoa 1 cup; Bell peppers 1 cup (sliced); Onion 1/2 cup (sliced); Cajun seasoning 2 Tbsp.; Olive oil 2 Tbsp.; Avocado 1 (sliced); Lime wedges for serving

DIRECTIONS: Cook quinoa; Sauté shrimp, bell peppers, onion with Cajun seasoning in oil; Serve over quinoa with avocado, lime.

N.V.: Calories: 380, Fat: 14 g, Carbohydrates: 38 g, Protein: 26 g, Sugar: 3 g, Sodium: 300 mg, Potassium: 780 mg, Cholesterol: 172 mg

ROSEMARY ORANGE GLAZED SALMON

PREP.T.: 10 min **C. T.:** 15 min

MODE OF COOKING: Broiling - **SERVINGS:** 4

INGREDIENTS: Salmon fillets 4; Orange juice 1/2 cup; Honey 2 Tbsp.; Soy sauce 1 Tbsp.; Rosemary 1 tsp (chopped); Garlic 1 clove (minced); Salt and pepper to taste

DIRECTIONS: Mix juice, honey, soy sauce, rosemary, garlic; Glaze salmon; Broil until cooked; Season with salt, pepper.

N.V.: Calories: 305, Fat: 13 g, Carbohydrates: 12 g, Protein: 34 g, Sugar: 10 g, Sodium: 320 mg, Potassium: 840 mg, Cholesterol: 85 mg

LIME CILANTRO TILAPIA TACOS

PREP.T.: 15 min **C. T.:** 10 min

MODE OF COOKING: Grilling - **SERVINGS:** 4

INGREDIENTS: Tilapia fillets 4; Lime 2 (juiced); Cilantro 1/4 cup (chopped); Cabbage 2 cups (shredded); Avocado cream 1/4 cup; Corn tortillas 8; Salt and pepper to taste

DIRECTIONS: Marinate tilapia in lime juice, cilantro; Grill; Assemble tacos with fish, cabbage, avocado cream in tortillas.

N.V.: Calories: 290, Fat: 9 g, Carbohydrates: 30 g, Protein: 25 g, Sugar: 2 g, Sodium: 210 mg, Potassium: 620 mg, Cholesterol: 55 mg

PARMESAN HERB CRUSTED HALIBUT

PREP.T.: 10 min **C. T.:** 15 min

MODE OF COOKING: Baking - **SERVINGS:** 4

INGREDIENTS: Halibut fillets 4; Parmesan cheese 1/2 cup (grated); Bread crumbs 1/2 cup; Parsley 2 Tbsp. (chopped); Lemon zest 1 tsp; Olive oil 2 Tbsp.; Salt and pepper to taste

DIRECTIONS: Mix Parmesan, bread crumbs, parsley, lemon zest; Coat halibut in oil, crust mixture; Bake at 400°F (204°C).

N.V.: Calories: 310, Fat: 10 g, Carbohydrates: 9 g, Protein: 45 g, Sugar: 0 g, Sodium: 390 mg, Potassium: 1020 mg, Cholesterol: 110 mg

SPICY GRILLED OCTOPUS

PREP.T.: 20 min (plus marinating) **C. T.:** 10 min

MODE OF COOKING: Grilling - **SERVINGS:** 4

INGREDIENTS: Octopus 1 lb (cleaned); Olive oil 3 Tbsp.; Lemon 1 (juiced); Garlic 2 cloves (minced); Red chili flakes 1 tsp; Salt and pepper to taste; Parsley 1 Tbsp. (chopped)

DIRECTIONS: Marinate octopus in lemon juice, olive oil, garlic, chili, salt, pepper; Grill until tender; Garnish with parsley.

N.V.: Calories: 200, Fat: 10 g, Carbohydrates: 5 g, Protein: 22 g, Sugar: 0 g, Sodium: 470 mg, Potassium: 750 mg, Cholesterol: 50 mg

HERB-INFUSED MUSSELS

PREP.T.: 10 min **C. T.:** 10 min

MODE OF COOKING: Steaming - **SERVINGS:** 4

INGREDIENTS: Mussels 2 lbs (cleaned); White wine 1 cup; Garlic 3 cloves (minced); Shallots 2 (chopped); Thyme 1 tsp; Parsley 2 Tbsp. (chopped); Butter 2 Tbsp.; Salt and pepper to taste

DIRECTIONS: Steam mussels with wine, garlic, shallots, thyme; Add butter, parsley at end; Season.

N.V.: Calories: 275, Fat: 10 g, Carbohydrates: 10 g, Protein: 28 g, Sugar: 0 g, Sodium: 705 mg, Potassium: 620 mg, Cholesterol: 78 mg

COCONUT SHRIMP CURRY

PREP.T.: 15 min **C. T.:** 20 min

MODE OF COOKING: Simmering - **SERVINGS:** 4

INGREDIENTS: Shrimp 1 lb (peeled); Coconut milk 1 can; Curry powder 2 Tbsp.; Onion 1 (diced); Tomato 1 cup (diced); Spinach 2 cups; Olive oil 1 Tbsp.; Salt and pepper to taste

DIRECTIONS: Sauté onion in oil; Add curry, coconut milk, tomato; Simmer; Add shrimp, cook until done; Stir in spinach.

N.V.: Calories: 350, Fat: 22 g, Carbohydrates: 12 g, Protein: 28 g, Sugar: 2 g, Sodium: 320 mg, Potassium: 630 mg, Cholesterol: 185 mg

FISH TACOS WITH MANGO SALSA

PREP.T.: 20 min **C. T.:** 10 min

MODE OF COOKING: Grilling - **SERVINGS:** 4

INGREDIENTS: White fish fillets 1 lb; Cabbage 2 cups (shredded); Mango 1 (diced); Red onion 1/4 cup (diced); Cilantro 1/4 cup (chopped); Lime 2 (juiced); Corn tortillas 8; Olive oil 2 Tbsp.; Salt and pepper to taste

DIRECTIONS: Grill fish with salt, pepper, lime juice; Mix mango, onion, cilantro for salsa; Serve fish in tortillas with cabbage, salsa.

N.V.: Calories: 300, Fat: 9 g, Carbohydrates: 35 g, Protein: 22 g, Sugar: 10 g, Sodium: 210 mg, Potassium: 590 mg, Cholesterol: 50 mg

LEMON BUTTER SCALLOPS WITH PARSLEY

PREP.T.: 5 min **C. T.:** 10 min

MODE OF COOKING: Sautéing - **SERVINGS:** 4

INGREDIENTS: Scallops 1 lb; Butter 3 Tbsp.; Lemon 1 (juiced); Parsley 2 Tbsp. (chopped); Garlic 1 clove (minced); Salt and pepper to taste

DIRECTIONS: Melt butter, add garlic; Sear scallops until golden; Remove, add lemon juice to pan; Pour over scallops, garnish with parsley.

N.V.: Calories: 215, Fat: 12 g, Carbohydrates: 5 g, Protein: 23 g, Sugar: 0 g, Sodium: 560 mg, Potassium: 380 mg, Cholesterol: 55 mg

CHAPTER 10: POULTRY AND BEAF RECIPES

Diving into the world of poultry and beef is like opening a gateway to a myriad of flavors, textures, and nutritional benefits that are both timeless and versatile. Chapter 10 is a culinary journey, guiding you through the art of transforming these staple proteins into dishes that resonate with the soulful warmth of home cooking while aligning with the Galveston Diet's principles for health and wellness. Here, we celebrate the lean, protein-rich profiles of chicken and turkey, alongside the robust, iron-packed essence of beef, showcasing how each can be the star of anti-inflammatory meals that don't just satisfy your hunger but nourish your body and support hormone balance. From the comforting embrace of a slow-cooked stew that simmers with depth and complexity, to the simple yet profound pleasure of a perfectly grilled steak or roast, each recipe is crafted to bring out the best in these ingredients, emphasizing their natural flavors while infusing them with a spectrum of spices, herbs, and nutritious sides.

Acknowledging the busy rhythms of modern life, this chapter is designed with both simplicity and splendor in mind. Whether you're gathering around the table for a family dinner, meal prepping for the week ahead, or seeking to impress guests at a gathering, these recipes offer solutions that are as practical as they are pleasing to the palate.

Embrace this chapter as your guide to exploring the rich potential of poultry and beef in your culinary repertoire, ensuring that every meal is an opportunity to feed your body, delight your senses, and cultivate a lifestyle of health and happiness.

ROSEMARY GARLIC CHICKEN BREASTS

PREP.T.: 10 min **C. T.:** 20 min
MODE OF COOKING: Roasting - **SERVINGS:** 4
INGREDIENTS: Chicken breasts 4; Olive oil 2 Tbsp.; Garlic 3 cloves (minced); Rosemary 2 tsp; Lemon juice 1 Tbsp.; Salt and pepper to taste
DIRECTIONS: Marinate chicken with all ingredients; Roast at 375°F (190°C) until fully cooked.
N.V.: Calories: 165, Fat: 5 g, Carbohydrates: 1 g, Protein: 26 g, Sugar: 0 g, Sodium: 320 mg, Potassium: 435 mg, Cholesterol: 65 mg

BALSAMIC GLAZED BEEF STEAK

PREP.T.: 10 min **C. T.:** 15 min

MODE OF COOKING: Grilling - **SERVINGS:** 4

INGREDIENTS: Beef steaks 4 (6 oz each); Balsamic vinegar 1/4 cup; Olive oil 2 Tbsp.; Garlic 2 cloves (minced); Thyme 1 tsp; Salt and pepper to taste

DIRECTIONS: Marinate steaks in vinegar, oil, garlic, thyme; Grill to desired doneness; Rest before serving.

N.V.: Calories: 290, Fat: 15 g, Carbohydrates: 3 g, Protein: 34 g, Sugar: 2 g, Sodium: 390 mg, Potassium: 510 mg, Cholesterol: 90 mg

TURKEY MEATBALLS WITH SPINACH

PREP.T.: 15 min **C. T.:** 20 min

MODE OF COOKING: Baking - **SERVINGS:** 4

INGREDIENTS: Ground turkey 1 lb; Spinach 1 cup (chopped); Onion 1/2 cup (minced); Egg 1; Bread crumbs 1/4 cup; Parmesan 2 Tbsp.; Salt and pepper to taste

DIRECTIONS: Combine all ingredients; Form into balls; Bake at 400°F (204°C) until browned and cooked through.

N.V.: Calories: 220, Fat: 9 g, Carbohydrates: 8 g, Protein: 28 g, Sugar: 2 g, Sodium: 420 mg, Potassium: 360 mg, Cholesterol: 120 mg

SPICY BEEF AND BROCCOLI STIR-FRY

PREP.T.: 10 min **C. T.:** 10 min

MODE OF COOKING: Stir-frying - **SERVINGS:** 4

INGREDIENTS: Beef sirloin 1 lb (thinly sliced); Broccoli 2 cups (florets); Soy sauce 1/4 cup; Garlic 2 cloves (minced); Ginger 1 tsp (grated); Red pepper flakes 1/2 tsp; Olive oil 2 Tbsp.; Salt to taste

DIRECTIONS: Stir-fry beef in oil, set aside; Cook broccoli; Add garlic, ginger; Return beef, add soy sauce, pepper flakes; Heat through.

N.V.: Calories: 250, Fat: 10 g, Carbohydrates: 10 g, Protein: 30 g, Sugar: 3 g, Sodium: 660 mg, Potassium: 640 mg, Cholesterol: 70 mg

HERBED CHICKEN PARMESAN

PREP.T.: 15 min **C. T.:** 20 min

MODE OF COOKING: Baking - **SERVINGS:** 4

INGREDIENTS: Chicken breasts 4; Bread crumbs 1/2 cup; Parmesan cheese 1/4 cup (grated); Basil 1 Tbsp. (chopped); Marinara sauce 1 cup; Mozzarella 1 cup (shredded); Olive oil 2 Tbsp.; Salt and pepper to taste

DIRECTIONS: Coat chicken in bread crumbs, Parmesan, basil; Bake halfway; Top with sauce, mozzarella; Finish baking until cheese melts.

N.V.: Calories: 340, Fat: 16 g, Carbohydrates: 12 g, Protein: 38 g, Sugar: 4 g, Sodium: 690 mg, Potassium: 470 mg, Cholesterol: 90 mg

SLOW-COOKED BEEF RAGU

PREP.T.: 20 min **C. T.:** 8 hr

MODE OF COOKING: Slow-cooking - **SERVINGS:** 6

INGREDIENTS: Beef chuck roast 2 lbs; Tomatoes 1 can (28 oz crushed); Onion 1 (chopped); Garlic 4 cloves (minced); Carrot 1 cup (diced); Red wine 1/2 cup; Thyme 1 tsp; Salt and pepper to taste

DIRECTIONS: Combine all ingredients in slow cooker; Cook on low until beef is tender; Shred beef, mix back into sauce.

N.V.: Calories: 310, Fat: 12 g, Carbohydrates: 9 g, Protein: 40 g, Sugar: 3 g, Sodium: 510 mg, Potassium: 840 mg, Cholesterol: 120 mg

GRILLED TURKEY BURGERS WITH AVOCADO

PREP.T.: 15 min **C. T.:** 10 min

MODE OF COOKING: Grilling - **SERVINGS:** 4

INGREDIENTS: Ground turkey 1 lb; Avocado 1 (mashed); Onion 1/4 cup (minced); Garlic 1 clove (minced); Cumin 1 tsp; Whole wheat buns 4; Lettuce, tomato for serving; Salt and pepper to taste

DIRECTIONS: Mix turkey, avocado, onion, garlic, cumin, salt, pepper; Form patties; Grill; Serve on buns with lettuce, tomato.

N.V.: Calories: 290, Fat: 14 g, Carbohydrates: 22 g, Protein: 21 g, Sugar: 3 g, Sodium: 320 mg, Potassium: 570 mg, Cholesterol: 80 mg

LEMON DILL ROAST CHICKEN

PREP.T.: 15 min **C. T.:** 1 hr 20 min

MODE OF COOKING: Roasting - **SERVINGS:** 4

INGREDIENTS: Whole chicken 4 lbs; Lemon 2 (sliced); Dill 1/4 cup (chopped); Butter 3 Tbsp. (melted); Garlic 4 cloves (minced); Salt and pepper to taste

DIRECTIONS: Stuff chicken with lemon slices, dill; Rub with butter, garlic, salt, pepper; Roast at 375°F (190°C) until golden.

N.V.: Calories: 410, Fat: 23 g, Carbohydrates: 3 g, Protein: 45 g, Sugar: 0 g, Sodium: 320 mg, Potassium: 370 mg, Cholesterol: 130 mg

BEEF STIR-FRY WITH BROCCOLI AND PEPPERS

PREP.T.: 15 min **C. T.:** 10 min

MODE OF COOKING: Stir-frying - **SERVINGS:** 4

INGREDIENTS: Beef strips 1 lb; Broccoli florets 2 cups; Red bell pepper 1 (sliced); Soy sauce 3 Tbsp.; Sesame oil 2 Tbsp.; Honey 1 Tbsp.; Garlic 2 cloves (minced); Ginger 1 Tbsp. (grated); Salt and pepper to taste

DIRECTIONS: Stir-fry beef in sesame oil; Add vegetables, garlic, ginger; Mix in soy sauce, honey; Cook until veggies are tender.

N.V.: Calories: 280, Fat: 12 g, Carbohydrates: 18 g, Protein: 26 g, Sugar: 8 g, Sodium: 660 mg, Potassium: 640 mg, Cholesterol: 70 mg

CHICKEN PICCATA WITH CAPERS

PREP.T.: 10 min **C. T.:** 20 min

MODE OF COOKING: Sautéing - **SERVINGS:** 4

INGREDIENTS: Chicken breast halves 4; Flour 1/4 cup; Butter 2 Tbsp.; Lemon juice 3 Tbsp.; Capers 2 Tbsp.; Chicken broth 1/2 cup; Parsley 1 Tbsp. (chopped); Salt and pepper to taste

DIRECTIONS: Dredge chicken in flour; Sauté in butter; Add lemon juice, capers, broth; Simmer; Garnish with parsley.

N.V.: Calories: 235, Fat: 8 g, Carbohydrates: 7 g, Protein: 34 g, Sugar: 0 g, Sodium: 410 mg, Potassium: 290 mg, Cholesterol: 95 mg

SLOW COOKER TURKEY CHILI

PREP.T.: 20 min **C. T.:** 6 hr

MODE OF COOKING: Slow-cooking - **SERVINGS:** 6

INGREDIENTS: Ground turkey 1 lb; Kidney beans 2 cups (drained); Tomato sauce 2 cups; Onion 1 (chopped); Chili powder 2 Tbsp.; Cumin 1 tsp; Garlic 2 cloves (minced); Salt and pepper to taste

DIRECTIONS: Combine all ingredients in slow cooker; Cook on low for 6 hours; Adjust seasoning as needed.

N.V.: Calories: 280, Fat: 6 g, Carbohydrates: 32 g, Protein: 27 g, Sugar: 6 g, Sodium: 720 mg, Potassium: 800 mg, Cholesterol: 70 mg

BALSAMIC BEEF SHORT RIBS

PREP.T.: 20 min **C. T.:** 3 hr

MODE OF COOKING: Braising - **SERVINGS:** 4

INGREDIENTS: Beef short ribs 2 lbs; Balsamic vinegar 1/2 cup; Beef broth 1 cup; Onion 1 (sliced); Garlic 4 cloves (minced); Rosemary 1 Tbsp.; Salt and pepper to taste

DIRECTIONS: Sear ribs; Remove; Sauté onion, garlic; Add vinegar, broth, rosemary; Return ribs; Cover, braise at 325°F (163°C).

N.V.: Calories: 480, Fat: 28 g, Carbohydrates: 12 g, Protein: 44 g, Sugar: 6 g, Sodium: 590 mg, Potassium: 610 mg, Cholesterol: 130 mg

GRILLED CHICKEN WITH MANGO SALSA

PREP.T.: 15 min **C. T.:** 15 min

MODE OF COOKING: Grilling - **SERVINGS:** 4

INGREDIENTS: Chicken breasts 4; Mango 1 (diced); Red bell pepper 1/2 (diced); Red onion 1/4 cup (diced); Cilantro 2 Tbsp. (chopped); Lime juice 2 Tbsp.; Chili powder 1 tsp; Salt and pepper to taste

DIRECTIONS: Season chicken with chili, salt, pepper; Grill; Combine mango, bell pepper, onion, cilantro, lime for salsa; Serve over chicken.

N.V.: Calories: 260, Fat: 3 g, Carbohydrates: 20 g, Protein: 35 g, Sugar: 15 g, Sodium: 320 mg, Potassium: 690 mg, Cholesterol: 85 mg

CHAPTER 11: SALADS RECIPES

Salads, often pigeonholed as mere sides or starters, emerge in this chapter as the stars of the culinary show, bursting with colors, textures, and flavors that can only be described as a feast for the senses. These aren't your ordinary salads; they're vibrant compositions that bring together the freshest of ingredients, each with their unique nutritional profiles, to create dishes that are as nourishing as they are delightful to the palate.

In the realm of the Galveston Diet, salads are celebrated not just for their ability to deliver a powerhouse of nutrients in every bite but also for their versatility and ease of preparation. This chapter is a homage to the art of salad-making, guiding you through a variety of recipes that range from hearty, meal-worthy bowls to light, refreshing sides perfect for any occasion. You'll discover how to balance flavors and textures, how to dress your salads for success with homemade dressings that ditch the processed additives in favor of natural, wholesome ingredients, and how to incorporate anti-inflammatory foods that support hormone balance and overall wellness.

Whether you're looking to brighten up your meals with a burst of antioxidants, seeking a satisfying yet light dinner option, or simply in need of inspiration to make greens and veggies a more prominent part of your diet, these salad recipes are your gateway to doing so with joy and creativity. Embrace the diversity of ingredients, the simplicity of preparation, and the sheer joy of eating something that looks just as beautiful as it tastes. Welcome to the chapter where salads take center stage, transforming the ordinary into the extraordinary.

SPINACH AND STRAWBERRY SALAD

PREP.T.: 10 min **C. T.:** 0 min

MODE OF COOKING: Tossing - **SERVINGS:** 4

INGREDIENTS: Spinach 4 cups; Strawberries 1 cup (sliced); Walnuts 1/2 cup (toasted); Goat cheese 1/4 cup (crumbled); Balsamic vinaigrette 3 Tbsp.

DIRECTIONS: Combine spinach, strawberries, walnuts, goat cheese in a bowl; Drizzle with vinaigrette; Toss gently.

N.V.: Calories: 180, Fat: 12 g, Carbohydrates: 12 g, Protein: 6 g, Sugar: 6 g, Sodium: 120 mg, Potassium: 320 mg, Cholesterol: 10 mg

QUINOA AND BLACK BEAN SALAD

PREP.T.: 15 min **C. T.:** 15 min

MODE OF COOKING: Boiling - **SERVINGS:** 4

INGREDIENTS: Quinoa 1 cup; Black beans 1 can (drained, rinsed); Corn 1 cup; Red bell pepper 1 (diced); Cilantro 1/4 cup (chopped); Lime dressing 3 Tbsp.

DIRECTIONS: Cook quinoa; Mix with beans, corn, pepper, cilantro; Add dressing; Chill before serving.

N.V.: Calories: 250, Fat: 5 g, Carbohydrates: 45 g, Protein: 10 g, Sugar: 2 g, Sodium: 300 mg, Potassium: 600 mg, Cholesterol: 0 mg

CAESAR SALAD WITH GRILLED CHICKEN

PREP.T.: 10 min **C. T.:** 10 min

MODE OF COOKING: Grilling - **SERVINGS:** 4

INGREDIENTS: Chicken breast 1 lb; Romaine lettuce 4 cups (chopped); Parmesan cheese 1/4 cup (shaved); Caesar dressing 1/4 cup; Croutons 1 cup

DIRECTIONS: Grill chicken, slice; Toss lettuce with dressing, cheese, croutons; Top with chicken.

N.V.: Calories: 320, Fat: 16 g, Carbohydrates: 12 g, Protein: 34 g, Sugar: 2 g, Sodium: 420 mg, Potassium: 300 mg, Cholesterol: 85 mg

AVOCADO AND GRAPEFRUIT SALAD

PREP.T.: 10 min **C. T.:** 0 min

MODE OF COOKING: Assembling - **SERVINGS:** 4

INGREDIENTS: Avocado 2 (sliced); Grapefruit 2 (segments); Mixed greens 4 cups; Red onion 1/4 cup (thinly sliced); Citrus vinaigrette 3 Tbsp.

DIRECTIONS: Arrange mixed greens, avocado, grapefruit, onion on plates; Drizzle with vinaigrette.

N.V.: Calories: 210, Fat: 15 g, Carbohydrates: 20 g, Protein: 3 g, Sugar: 12 g, Sodium: 60 mg, Potassium: 560 mg, Cholesterol: 0 mg

---

BEET AND GOAT CHEESE ARUGULA SALAD

PREP.T.: 15 min **C. T.:** 0 min

MODE OF COOKING: Assembling - **SERVINGS:** 4

INGREDIENTS: Arugula 4 cups; Beets 1 cup (cooked, sliced); Goat cheese 1/3 cup (crumbled); Walnuts 1/2 cup (toasted); Honey vinaigrette 3 Tbsp.

DIRECTIONS: Layer arugula, beets, goat cheese, walnuts on plates; Drizzle with vinaigrette.

N.V.: Calories: 220, Fat: 16 g, Carbohydrates: 14 g, Protein: 8 g, Sugar: 10 g, Sodium: 180 mg, Potassium: 380 mg, Cholesterol: 15 mg

---

SUMMER BERRY SALAD WITH POPPY SEED DRESSING

PREP.T.: 10 min **C. T.:** 0 min

MODE OF COOKING: Tossing - **SERVINGS:** 4

INGREDIENTS: Mixed greens 4 cups; Strawberries 1 cup (sliced); Blueberries 1 cup; Almonds 1/4 cup (sliced); Feta cheese 1/4 cup (crumbled); Poppy seed dressing 3 Tbsp.

DIRECTIONS: Combine all ingredients in a large bowl; Toss with dressing.

N.V.: Calories: 190, Fat: 12 g, Carbohydrates: 17 g, Protein: 5 g, Sugar: 11 g, Sodium: 220 mg, Potassium: 270 mg, Cholesterol: 15 mg

---

ASIAN CHICKEN SALAD

PREP.T.: 20 min **C. T.:** 0 min

MODE OF COOKING: Tossing - **SERVINGS:** 4

INGREDIENTS: Chicken breast 1 lb (cooked, shredded); Cabbage 2 cups (shredded); Carrot 1 cup (shredded); Red bell pepper 1 (thinly sliced); Almonds 1/4 cup (toasted); Sesame seeds 1 Tbsp.; Asian dressing 1/4 cup

DIRECTIONS: Combine chicken, vegetables, almonds, sesame seeds; Add dressing; Toss well.

N.V.: Calories: 250, Fat: 12 g, Carbohydrates: 10 g, Protein: 26 g, Sugar: 5 g, Sodium: 300 mg, Potassium: 400 mg, Cholesterol: 60 mg

CRUNCHY CABBAGE AND CARROT SLAW

PREP.T.: 15 min **C. T.:** 0 min

MODE OF COOKING: Mixing - **SERVINGS:** 4

INGREDIENTS: Cabbage 2 cups (shredded); Carrot 1 cup (shredded); Green onions 1/4 cup (sliced); Almonds 1/4 cup (toasted); Apple cider vinegar 2 Tbsp.; Olive oil 1 Tbsp.; Honey 1 tsp; Salt and pepper to taste

DIRECTIONS: Toss cabbage, carrot, green onions, almonds; Whisk vinegar, oil, honey; Dress salad; Season.

N.V.: Calories: 120, Fat: 7 g, Carbohydrates: 12 g, Protein: 2 g, Sugar: 7 g, Sodium: 75 mg, Potassium: 210 mg, Cholesterol: 0 mg

PEAR AND GORGONZOLA SALAD

PREP.T.: 10 min **C. T.:** 0 min

MODE OF COOKING: Assembling - **SERVINGS:** 4

INGREDIENTS: Mixed greens 4 cups; Pear 1 (sliced); Gorgonzola 1/4 cup (crumbled); Walnuts 1/4 cup (toasted); Balsamic vinaigrette 3 Tbsp.

DIRECTIONS: Arrange greens, pear slices, Gorgonzola, walnuts on plates; Drizzle with vinaigrette.

N.V.: Calories: 180, Fat: 12 g, Carbohydrates: 15 g, Protein: 4 g, Sugar: 10 g, Sodium: 220 mg, Potassium: 180 mg, Cholesterol: 15 mg

SOUTHWESTERN QUINOA SALAD

PREP.T.: 20 min **C. T.:** 15 min

MODE OF COOKING: Boiling - **SERVINGS:** 4

INGREDIENTS: Quinoa 1 cup; Black beans 1 can (drained, rinsed); Corn 1 cup; Avocado 1 (diced); Tomato 1 cup (diced); Lime juice 2 Tbsp.; Cilantro 1/4 cup (chopped); Chili powder 1 tsp; Salt to taste

DIRECTIONS: Cook quinoa; Cool; Mix with beans, corn, avocado, tomato; Add lime juice, cilantro, chili powder; Season.

N.V.: Calories: 310, Fat: 8 g, Carbohydrates: 50 g, Protein: 12 g, Sugar: 4 g, Sodium: 300 mg, Potassium: 720 mg, Cholesterol: 0 mg

WATERMELON AND FETA SALAD

PREP.T.: 10 min **C. T.:** 0 min

MODE OF COOKING: Tossing - **SERVINGS:** 4

INGREDIENTS: Watermelon 4 cups (cubed); Feta cheese 1 cup (crumbled); Mint 1/4 cup (chopped); Lime juice 2 Tbsp.; Olive oil 1 Tbsp.; Salt and pepper to taste

DIRECTIONS: Combine watermelon, feta, mint; Dress with lime juice, olive oil; Season lightly.

N.V.: Calories: 200, Fat: 10 g, Carbohydrates: 25 g, Protein: 7 g, Sugar: 20 g, Sodium: 320 mg, Potassium: 270 mg, Cholesterol: 25 mg

CLASSIC GREEK SALAD

PREP.T.: 10 min **C. T.:** 0 min

MODE OF COOKING: Mixing - **SERVINGS:** 4

INGREDIENTS: Cucumber 2 cups (diced); Tomato 2 cups (diced); Red onion 1/4 cup (sliced); Kalamata olives 1/4 cup; Feta cheese 1 cup (cubed); Olive oil 3 Tbsp.; Red wine vinegar 1 Tbsp.; Oregano 1 tsp; Salt and pepper to taste

DIRECTIONS: Toss cucumber, tomato, onion, olives, feta; Dress with oil, vinegar, oregano; Season.

N.V.: Calories: 220, Fat: 16 g, Carbohydrates: 12 g, Protein: 7 g, Sugar: 5 g, Sodium: 420 mg, Potassium: 360 mg, Cholesterol: 25 mg

ROASTED BEET AND WALNUT SALAD

PREP.T.: 15 min **C. T.:** 1 hr (for beets)

MODE OF COOKING: Roasting - **SERVINGS:** 4

INGREDIENTS: Beets 4 (roasted, peeled, sliced); Walnuts 1/2 cup (toasted); Goat cheese 1/4 cup (crumbled); Mixed greens 4 cups; Orange vinaigrette 3 Tbsp.

DIRECTIONS: Arrange mixed greens, beets, walnuts, goat cheese on plates; Drizzle with vinaigrette.

N.V.: Calories: 210, Fat: 14 g, Carbohydrates: 16 g, Protein: 6 g, Sugar: 11 g, Sodium: 180 mg, Potassium: 400 mg, Cholesterol: 10 mg

CHAPTER 12: VEGETARIAN RECIPES

Venturing into the realm of vegetarian cuisine opens up a world of vibrant flavors, rich nutrients, and endless creativity. In this chapter, we'll explore the depth and diversity of vegetarian cooking, showcasing recipes that make the most of fresh, whole-food ingredients. These dishes are designed not only to nourish the body and delight the palate but also to align with the principles of the Galveston Diet, emphasizing anti-inflammatory benefits and hormone balance.

Each recipe is a celebration of the earth's bounty, featuring a variety of vegetables, fruits, whole grains, and legumes, all playing their part in creating meals that are as satisfying as they are healthful. From hearty entrees that comfort and fill, to light and refreshing sides perfect for any occasion, these vegetarian recipes offer something for every taste and preference.

Beyond their nutritional value, these recipes are about embracing a style of eating that respects the body and the planet. They are crafted to be accessible, using ingredients that are readily available and techniques that are practical for cooks of all levels. Whether you're a long-time vegetarian or simply looking to incorporate more plant-based meals into your diet, this chapter provides the inspiration and guidance you need to explore the delightful possibilities of vegetarian cooking.

Prepare to be surprised by the depth of flavors and textures that vegetarian cuisine has to offer. Let these recipes be your guide to a world where eating healthfully doesn't mean sacrificing taste or satisfaction. Welcome to the vibrant heart of vegetarian cooking, where every dish is a step towards a healthier, more balanced lifestyle.

ROASTED CAULIFLOWER STEAKS

PREP.T.: 5 min **C. T.:** 25 min

MODE OF COOKING: Roasting - **SERVINGS:** 4

INGREDIENTS: Cauliflower 2 heads (sliced into steaks); Olive oil 2 Tbsp.; Garlic powder 1 tsp; Paprika 1 tsp; Salt and pepper to taste

DIRECTIONS: Brush cauliflower steaks with oil, season; Roast at 400°F (204°C) until tender and golden.

N.V.: Calories: 120, Fat: 7 g, Carbohydrates: 11 g, Protein: 4 g, Sugar: 4 g, Sodium: 60 mg, Potassium: 640 mg, Cholesterol: 0 mg

---

SPINACH AND RICOTTA STUFFED SHELLS

PREP.T.: 20 min **C. T.:** 25 min

MODE OF COOKING: Baking - **SERVINGS:** 4

INGREDIENTS: Jumbo pasta shells 20; Ricotta cheese 1 cup; Spinach 1 cup (cooked, squeezed dry); Mozzarella cheese 1/2 cup (shredded); Marinara sauce 2 cups; Salt and pepper to taste

DIRECTIONS: Fill cooked shells with ricotta, spinach; Top with sauce, mozzarella; Bake at 375°F (190°C).

N.V.: Calories: 350, Fat: 14 g, Carbohydrates: 40 g, Protein: 18 g, Sugar: 5 g, Sodium: 480 mg, Potassium: 410 mg, Cholesterol: 30 mg

---

SWEET POTATO AND BLACK BEAN BURGERS

PREP.T.: 15 min **C. T.:** 40 min

MODE OF COOKING: Baking - **SERVINGS:** 4

INGREDIENTS: Sweet potatoes 2 (cooked, mashed); Black beans 1 cup (mashed); Quinoa 1/2 cup (cooked); Cumin 1 tsp; Paprika 1 tsp; Salt and pepper to taste; Whole wheat buns 4

DIRECTIONS: Mix ingredients; Form patties; Bake at 375°F (190°C) until firm; Serve on buns.

N.V.: Calories: 290, Fat: 2 g, Carbohydrates: 60 g, Protein: 10 g, Sugar: 8 g, Sodium: 320 mg, Potassium: 670 mg, Cholesterol: 0 mg

---

GRILLED EGGPLANT WITH TOMATO AND FETA

PREP.T.: 10 min **C. T.:** 10 min

MODE OF COOKING: Grilling - **SERVINGS:** 4

INGREDIENTS: Eggplant 2 (sliced); Olive oil 2 Tbsp.; Tomato 2 (sliced); Feta cheese 1/2 cup (crumbled); Balsamic glaze 2 Tbsp.; Basil leaves 1/4 cup

DIRECTIONS: Brush eggplant with oil; Grill; Layer with tomato, feta; Drizzle with balsamic; Garnish with basil.

N.V.: Calories: 180, Fat: 12 g, Carbohydrates: 15 g, Protein: 5 g, Sugar: 9 g, Sodium: 320 mg, Potassium: 520 mg, Cholesterol: 25 mg

---

CHICKPEA AND AVOCADO SALAD

PREP.T.: 10 min **C. T.:** 0 min

MODE OF COOKING: Mixing - **SERVINGS:** 4

INGREDIENTS: Chickpeas 1 can (drained, rinsed); Avocado 2 (diced); Red onion 1/4 cup (finely chopped); Cilantro 1/4 cup (chopped); Lime 1 (juiced); Olive oil 1 Tbsp.; Salt and pepper to taste

DIRECTIONS: Mix all ingredients gently; Chill before serving.

N.V.: Calories: 240, Fat: 14 g, Carbohydrates: 24 g, Protein: 7 g, Sugar: 3 g, Sodium: 320 mg, Potassium: 590 mg, Cholesterol: 0 mg

---

BUTTERNUT SQUASH AND QUINOA PILAF

PREP.T.: 15 min **C. T.:** 30 min

MODE OF COOKING: Roasting/Simmering - **SERVINGS:** 4

INGREDIENTS: Butternut squash 2 cups (cubed); Quinoa 1 cup; Vegetable broth 2 cups; Cranberries 1/2 cup (dried); Walnuts 1/2 cup (toasted); Olive oil 2 Tbsp.; Sage 1 tsp (chopped); Salt and pepper to taste

DIRECTIONS: Roast squash; Simmer quinoa in broth; Combine all with cranberries, walnuts, sage.

N.V.: Calories: 320, Fat: 14 g, Carbohydrates: 45 g, Protein: 8 g, Sugar: 8 g, Sodium: 480 mg, Potassium: 670 mg, Cholesterol: 0 mg

---

MUSHROOM STROGANOFF

PREP.T.: 10 min **C. T.:** 20 min

MODE OF COOKING: Sautéing - **SERVINGS:** 4

INGREDIENTS: Mushrooms 2 cups (sliced); Onion 1 (chopped); Garlic 2 cloves (minced); Vegetable broth 2 cups; Sour cream 1/2 cup; Flour 2 Tbsp.; Paprika 1 tsp; Whole wheat pasta 8 oz; Parsley 1/4 cup (chopped); Salt and pepper to taste

DIRECTIONS: Sauté mushrooms, onion, garlic; Add flour, paprika, broth; Simmer; Mix in sour cream; Serve over pasta; Garnish with parsley.

N.V.: Calories: 300, Fat: 7 g, Carbohydrates: 50 g, Protein: 10 g, Sugar: 5 g, Sodium: 240 mg, Potassium: 640 mg, Cholesterol: 20 mg

LENTIL TACOS WITH AVOCADO CILANTRO SAUCE

PREP.T.: 15 min **C. T.:** 25 min

MODE OF COOKING: Simmering - **SERVINGS:** 4

INGREDIENTS: Lentils 1 cup; Vegetable broth 2 cups; Taco seasoning 1 Tbsp.; Avocado 1; Cilantro 1/2 cup; Lime 1 (juiced); Garlic 1 clove; Corn tortillas 8; Salt and pepper to taste

DIRECTIONS: Cook lentils in broth with seasoning; Blend avocado, cilantro, lime, garlic for sauce; Serve lentils on tortillas with sauce.

N.V.: Calories: 280, Fat: 7 g, Carbohydrates: 45 g, Protein: 12 g, Sugar: 2 g, Sodium: 300 mg, Potassium: 720 mg, Cholesterol: 0 mg

CAULIFLOWER BUFFALO WINGS

PREP.T.: 15 min **C. T.:** 25 min

MODE OF COOKING: Baking - **SERVINGS:** 4

INGREDIENTS: Cauliflower 1 head (cut into florets); Flour 1 cup; Almond milk 1 cup; Garlic powder 1 tsp; Paprika 1 tsp; Buffalo sauce 1/2 cup; Salt and pepper to taste

DIRECTIONS: Batter cauliflower with flour, milk, spices; Bake at 450°F (232°C); Toss with buffalo sauce; Bake again until crispy.

N.V.: Calories: 180, Fat: 2 g, Carbohydrates: 35 g, Protein: 6 g, Sugar: 4 g, Sodium: 880 mg, Potassium: 430 mg, Cholesterol: 0 mg

VEGAN MUSHROOM BOURGUIGNON

PREP.T.: 20 min **C. T.:** 40 min

MODE OF COOKING: Simmering - **SERVINGS:** 4

INGREDIENTS: Mushrooms 3 cups (sliced); Onion 1 (chopped); Carrot 1 (diced); Garlic 2 cloves (minced); Red wine 1 cup; Vegetable broth 2 cups; Tomato paste 2 Tbsp.; Thyme 1 tsp; Whole wheat flour 2 Tbsp.; Olive oil 2 Tbsp.; Salt and pepper to taste

DIRECTIONS: Sauté mushrooms, onion, carrot, garlic in oil; Add flour, stir; Add wine, broth, tomato paste, thyme; Simmer until thick.

N.V.: Calories: 250, Fat: 7 g, Carbohydrates: 35 g, Protein: 6 g, Sugar: 6 g, Sodium: 480 mg, Potassium: 750 mg, Cholesterol: 0 mg

---

SPICY THAI PEANUT SWEET POTATO BOWL

PREP.T.: 15 min **C. T.:** 30 min

MODE OF COOKING: Roasting/Boiling - **SERVINGS:** 4

INGREDIENTS: Sweet potatoes 2 (cubed); Quinoa 1 cup; Spinach 2 cups; Peanut butter 1/4 cup; Soy sauce 2 Tbsp.; Lime 1 (juiced); Honey 1 Tbsp.; Garlic 1 clove (minced); Ginger 1 tsp (grated); Crushed red pepper 1/2 tsp; Water 2 Tbsp.; Salt and pepper to taste

DIRECTIONS: Roast sweet potatoes; Cook quinoa; Sauté spinach; Whisk peanut butter, soy sauce, lime juice, honey, garlic, ginger, red pepper, water for sauce; Combine.

N.V.: Calories: 380, Fat: 12 g, Carbohydrates: 60 g, Protein: 12 g, Sugar: 10 g, Sodium: 620 mg, Potassium: 1020 mg, Cholesterol: 0 mg

---

EGGPLANT PARMESAN CASSEROLE

PREP.T.: 20 min **C. T.:** 45 min

MODE OF COOKING: Baking - **SERVINGS:** 4

INGREDIENTS: Eggplant 2 (sliced); Marinara sauce 2 cups; Mozzarella cheese 1 cup (shredded); Parmesan cheese 1/2 cup (grated); Bread crumbs 1 cup; Eggs 2; Flour 1/2 cup; Olive oil for frying; Salt and pepper to taste

DIRECTIONS: Bread eggplant slices in flour, egg, breadcrumbs; Fry; Layer with sauce, cheeses in casserole; Bake at 375°F (190°C).

N.V.: Calories: 350, Fat: 18 g, Carbohydrates: 35 g, Protein: 16 g, Sugar: 8 g, Sodium: 680 mg, Potassium: 550 mg, Cholesterol: 110 mg

---

CHICKPEA SPINACH STUFFED PORTOBELLO MUSHROOMS

PREP.T.: 15 min **C. T.:** 25 min

MODE OF COOKING: Baking - **SERVINGS:** 4

INGREDIENTS: Portobello mushrooms 4; Chickpeas 1 can (drained, rinsed); Spinach 2 cups; Garlic 2 cloves (minced); Feta cheese 1/2 cup (crumbled); Olive oil 2 Tbsp.; Balsamic vinegar 1 Tbsp.; Salt and pepper to taste

DIRECTIONS: Scoop mushrooms; Sauté chickpeas, spinach, garlic; Stuff mushrooms; Top with feta; Drizzle with oil, vinegar; Bake at 375°F (190°C).

N.V.: Calories: 220, Fat: 12 g, Carbohydrates: 20 g, Protein: 10 g, Sugar: 4 g, Sodium: 320 mg, Potassium: 430 mg, Cholesterol: 25 mg

CHAPTER 13: SOUP AND STEW RECIPES

In the heart of every home kitchen lies the soulful comfort of soups and stews—timeless dishes that have the power to warm the body, soothe the mind, and nurture the soul. Chapter 13 is a loving ode to these culinary staples, a collection of recipes that simmer with tradition, innovation, and the pure joy of cooking. As we delve into the pages of this chapter, we're not just exploring a range of flavors and ingredients; we're embarking on a journey that connects us to the very essence of nourishment and well-being.

These recipes are carefully crafted to align with the principles of the Galveston Diet, emphasizing anti-inflammatory ingredients and hormone-balancing nutrients without sacrificing depth of flavor or heartiness. From the rustic elegance of a chunky vegetable stew that celebrates the bounty of the garden, to the refined simplicity of a broth-based soup that sings with clarity and spice, each recipe is designed to be both a delight to the senses and a boon to health.

Whether you're seeking the comforting embrace of a familiar classic or the thrill of a new and exotic blend, this chapter offers a sanctuary of choices. These soups and stews are more than just meals; they are a testament to the power of food to heal, connect, and comfort us through every season of life.

Join us at the table, where the steam rises in welcoming curls from the bowl, where every spoonful is a reminder of the simplicity and richness of eating well. Welcome to the chapter where each recipe is a warm embrace, inviting you to savor the art of cooking from the heart.

CLASSIC TOMATO BASIL SOUP

PREP.T.: 10 min **C. T.:** 30 min

MODE OF COOKING: Simmering - **SERVINGS:** 4

INGREDIENTS: Tomatoes 4 cups (crushed); Vegetable broth 2 cups; Onion 1 (chopped); Garlic 2 cloves (minced); Basil 1/4 cup (fresh, chopped); Olive oil 2 Tbsp.; Salt and pepper to taste

DIRECTIONS: Sauté onion, garlic in oil; Add tomatoes, broth; Simmer; Add basil; Blend until smooth.

N.V.: Calories: 90, Fat: 5 g, Carbohydrates: 11 g, Protein: 2 g, Sugar: 6 g, Sodium: 480 mg, Potassium: 430 mg, Cholesterol: 0 mg

LENTIL VEGETABLE STEW

PREP.T.: 15 min **C. T.:** 45 min

MODE OF COOKING: Simmering -

SERVINGS: 4

INGREDIENTS: Lentils 1 cup; Carrots 2 (diced); Celery 2 stalks (diced); Onion 1 (diced); Tomatoes 2 cups (diced); Vegetable broth 4 cups; Thyme 1 tsp; Salt and pepper to taste

DIRECTIONS: Combine all ingredients in pot; Simmer until lentils are tender.

N.V.: Calories: 240, Fat: 1 g, Carbohydrates: 45 g, Protein: 14 g, Sugar: 9 g, Sodium: 240 mg, Potassium: 710 mg, Cholesterol: 0 mg

BUTTERNUT SQUASH SOUP

PREP.T.: 20 min **C. T.:** 40 min

MODE OF COOKING: Blending - **SERVINGS:** 4

INGREDIENTS: Butternut squash 4 cups (cubed); Onion 1 (chopped); Vegetable broth 3 cups; Nutmeg 1/4 tsp; Cinnamon 1/4 tsp; Coconut milk 1 cup; Salt and pepper to taste

DIRECTIONS: Roast squash; Sauté onion; Combine squash, onion, broth, spices; Cook; Blend; Stir in coconut milk.

N.V.: Calories: 180, Fat: 9 g, Carbohydrates: 27 g, Protein: 3 g, Sugar: 6 g, Sodium: 58 mg, Potassium: 789 mg, Cholesterol: 0 mg

CHICKPEA AND SPINACH STEW

PREP.T.: 10 min **C. T.:** 20 min

MODE OF COOKING: Simmering - **SERVINGS:** 4

INGREDIENTS: Chickpeas 2 cups (drained); Spinach 2 cups; Tomatoes 2 cups (diced); Onion 1 (chopped); Garlic 2 cloves (minced); Cumin 1 tsp; Vegetable broth 2 cups; Olive oil 2 Tbsp.; Salt and pepper to taste

DIRECTIONS: Sauté onion, garlic in oil; Add chickpeas, tomatoes, cumin; Add broth; Simmer; Add spinach.

N.V.: Calories: 220, Fat: 7 g, Carbohydrates: 33 g, Protein: 9 g, Sugar: 6 g, Sodium: 480 mg, Potassium: 720 mg, Cholesterol: 0 mg

MUSHROOM BARLEY SOUP

PREP.T.: 15 min **C. T.:** 1 hr

MODE OF COOKING: Simmering - **SERVINGS:** 4

INGREDIENTS: Barley 1 cup; Mushrooms 2 cups (sliced); Carrots 1 cup (diced); Onion 1 (diced); Vegetable broth 4 cups; Thyme 1 tsp; Olive oil 2 Tbsp.; Salt and pepper to taste

DIRECTIONS: Sauté mushrooms, carrots, onion in oil; Add barley, broth, thyme; Simmer until barley is tender.

N.V.: Calories: 200, Fat: 7 g, Carbohydrates: 31 g, Protein: 6 g, Sugar: 4 g, Sodium: 240 mg, Potassium: 430 mg, Cholesterol: 0 mg

SPICY BLACK BEAN SOUP

PREP.T.: 10 min **C. T.:** 30 min

MODE OF COOKING: Simmering - **SERVINGS:** 4

INGREDIENTS: Black beans 2 cans (drained, rinsed); Onion 1 (chopped); Garlic 3 cloves (minced); Cumin 2 tsp; Vegetable broth 4 cups; Jalapeño 1 (minced); Lime 1 (juiced); Salt and pepper to taste

DIRECTIONS: Sauté onion, garlic, jalapeño; Add beans, cumin, broth; Simmer; Puree half; Add lime juice.

N.V.: Calories: 220, Fat: 1 g, Carbohydrates: 40 g, Protein: 14 g, Sugar: 2 g, Sodium: 260 mg, Potassium: 830 mg, Cholesterol: 0 mg

CREAMY POTATO LEEK SOUP

PREP.T.: 15 min **C. T.:** 30 min

MODE OF COOKING: Simmering - **SERVINGS:** 4

INGREDIENTS: Potatoes 4 cups (cubed); Leeks 3 (sliced, white and light green parts only); Vegetable broth 4 cups; Thyme 1 tsp; Cream 1 cup; Olive oil 2 Tbsp.; Salt and pepper to taste

DIRECTIONS: Sauté leeks in oil; Add potatoes, thyme, broth; Cook until tender; Blend until smooth; Stir in cream.

N.V.: Calories: 310, Fat: 19 g, Carbohydrates: 34 g, Protein: 4 g, Sugar: 4 g, Sodium: 240 mg, Potassium: 750 mg, Cholesterol: 55 mg

MOROCCAN LENTIL AND VEGETABLE STEW

PREP.T.: 20 min **C. T.:** 40 min

MODE OF COOKING: Simmering - **SERVINGS:** 4

INGREDIENTS: Lentils 1 cup; Carrots 2 (diced); Zucchini 2 cups (diced); Tomatoes 2 cups (diced); Onion 1 (chopped); Garlic 2 cloves (minced); Cumin 1 tsp; Cinnamon 1/2 tsp; Vegetable broth 4 cups; Cilantro 1/4 cup (chopped); Salt and pepper to taste

DIRECTIONS: Sauté onion, garlic, spices; Add lentils, vegetables, broth; Simmer until lentils are tender; Garnish with cilantro.

N.V.: Calories: 230, Fat: 1 g, Carbohydrates: 45 g, Protein: 14 g, Sugar: 8 g, Sodium: 300 mg, Potassium: 780 mg, Cholesterol: 0 mg

ROASTED RED PEPPER AND TOMATO SOUP

PREP.T.: 10 min **C. T.:** 45 min

MODE OF COOKING: Roasting/Blending - **SERVINGS:** 4

INGREDIENTS: Red peppers 4 (roasted, peeled); Tomatoes 4 cups (crushed); Onion 1 (chopped); Garlic 2 cloves (minced); Vegetable broth 2 cups; Basil 1/4 cup (fresh, chopped); Olive oil 2 Tbsp.; Salt and pepper to taste

DIRECTIONS: Sauté onion, garlic in oil; Add peppers, tomatoes, broth; Simmer; Blend until smooth; Stir in basil.

N.V.: Calories: 130, Fat: 7 g, Carbohydrates: 16 g, Protein: 3 g, Sugar: 9 g, Sodium: 240 mg, Potassium: 510 mg, Cholesterol: 0 mg

CURRIED BUTTERNUT SQUASH SOUP

PREP.T.: 15 min **C. T.:** 30 min

MODE OF COOKING: Simmering - **SERVINGS:** 4

INGREDIENTS: Butternut squash 3 cups (cubed); Onion 1 (chopped); Garlic 1 clove (minced); Curry powder 2 tsp; Coconut milk 1 cup; Vegetable broth 3 cups; Olive oil 1 Tbsp.; Salt to taste

DIRECTIONS: Sauté onion, garlic, curry; Add squash, broth; Simmer until soft; Blend; Stir in coconut milk.

N.V.: Calories: 220, Fat: 14 g, Carbohydrates: 24 g, Protein: 3 g, Sugar: 5 g, Sodium: 150 mg, Potassium: 670 mg, Cholesterol: 0 mg

WHITE BEAN AND KALE STEW

PREP.T.: 10 min **C. T.:** 30 min

MODE OF COOKING: Simmering - **SERVINGS:** 4

INGREDIENTS: White beans 2 cans (drained, rinsed); Kale 2 cups (torn); Carrots 1 cup (diced); Onion 1 (chopped); Vegetable broth 4 cups; Thyme 1 tsp; Olive oil 2 Tbsp.; Salt and pepper to taste

DIRECTIONS: Sauté onion, carrots in oil; Add beans, kale, broth, thyme; Simmer until vegetables are tender.

N.V.: Calories: 240, Fat: 5 g, Carbohydrates: 40 g, Protein: 12 g, Sugar: 3 g, Sodium: 300 mg, Potassium: 1010 mg, Cholesterol: 0 mg

HEARTY VEGETARIAN CHILI

PREP.T.: 20 min **C. T.:** 1 hr

MODE OF COOKING: Simmering - **SERVINGS:** 6

INGREDIENTS: Kidney beans 2 cans (drained, rinsed); Black beans 1 can (drained, rinsed); Crushed tomatoes 2 cups; Bell peppers 2 (diced); Onion 1 (chopped); Garlic 3 cloves (minced); Chili powder 2 Tbsp.; Cumin 1 tsp; Olive oil 2 Tbsp.; Salt and pepper to taste

DIRECTIONS: Sauté onion, garlic, peppers in oil; Add beans, tomatoes, spices; Simmer; Adjust seasoning.

N.V.: Calories: 250, Fat: 4 g, Carbohydrates: 45 g, Protein: 14 g, Sugar: 6 g, Sodium: 400 mg, Potassium: 960 mg, Cholesterol: 0 mg

PUMPKIN AND SAGE SOUP

PREP.T.: 15 min **C. T.:** 30 min

MODE OF COOKING: Blending - **SERVINGS:** 4

INGREDIENTS: Pumpkin puree 4 cups; Onion 1 (chopped); Garlic 1 clove (minced); Sage 1 Tbsp. (chopped); Vegetable broth 4 cups; Coconut milk 1 cup; Olive oil 1 Tbsp.; Salt and pepper to taste

DIRECTIONS: Sauté onion, garlic in oil; Add pumpkin, sage, broth; Simmer; Blend; Stir in coconut milk.

N.V.: Calories: 200, Fat: 12 g, Carbohydrates: 22 g, Protein: 3 g, Sugar: 5 g, Sodium: 100 mg, Potassium: 550 mg, Cholesterol: 0 mg

SWEET CORN AND POTATO CHOWDER

PREP.T.: 15 min **C. T.:** 25 min

MODE OF COOKING: Simmering - **SERVINGS:** 4

INGREDIENTS: Corn 2 cups (kernels); Potatoes 2 cups (cubed); Onion 1 (chopped); Vegetable broth 3 cups; Milk 1 cup; Thyme 1 tsp; Olive oil 1 Tbsp.; Salt and pepper to taste

DIRECTIONS: Sauté onion in oil; Add potatoes, corn, broth; Simmer until potatoes are soft; Add milk, thyme; Heat through.

N.V.: Calories: 230, Fat: 7 g, Carbohydrates: 38 g, Protein: 6 g, Sugar: 9 g, Sodium: 150 mg, Potassium: 720 mg, Cholesterol: 5 mg

ITALIAN BARLEY AND VEGETABLE SOUP

PREP.T.: 10 min **C. T.:** 40 min

MODE OF COOKING: Simmering - **SERVINGS:** 4

INGREDIENTS: Barley 1 cup; Carrots 1 cup (diced); Celery 1 cup (diced); Onion 1 (chopped); Zucchini 1 cup (diced); Diced tomatoes 2 cups; Vegetable broth 6 cups; Basil 1 Tbsp. (chopped); Olive oil 2 Tbsp.; Salt and pepper to taste

DIRECTIONS: Sauté onion, carrots, celery in oil; Add barley, broth, tomatoes; Simmer until barley is tender; Add zucchini, basil; Cook until zucchini is tender.

N.V.: Calories: 250, Fat: 7 g, Carbohydrates: 42 g, Protein: 6 g, Sugar: 6 g, Sodium: 300 mg, Potassium: 600 mg, Cholesterol: 0 mg

CHAPTER 14: SPECIAL OCCASIONS AND ENTERTAINING WITH EASE

Entertaining is an art form that combines the joy of gathering with the love of sharing meals, and in Chapter 14, we dive into the heart of special occasions and entertaining with ease. This chapter is dedicated to those moments that call for something a bit more extraordinary—a collection of recipes designed to dazzle your guests while still embracing the principles of the Galveston Diet. Whether you're hosting a festive holiday dinner, a casual weekend brunch, or an elegant cocktail party, these dishes are crafted to impress without leaving you overwhelmed in the kitchen.

The focus here is on balance—recipes that are both luxurious and healthful, indulgent yet in line with anti-inflammatory eating. We'll explore a variety of flavors and textures, from succulent mains and sophisticated sides to divine desserts and refreshing drinks, all designed to make your gatherings memorable and manageable. These dishes not only cater to the senses but also to the well-being of your guests, ensuring that everyone leaves the table feeling nourished and satisfied.

Moreover, this chapter is imbued with tips and strategies for seamless planning and preparation, allowing you to enjoy the celebration as much as your guests. Because true hospitality is about warmth and connection, not just the food on the table. So, let's embrace the joy of entertaining, armed with recipes that promise to make every occasion special, proving that you can entertain with elegance and ease while staying true to the principles of healthful eating. Welcome to the celebration—where every dish tells a story, and every gathering is an opportunity to nourish and delight.

QUINOA STUFFED BELL PEPPERS

PREP.T.: 20 min **C. T.:** 40 min
MODE OF COOKING: Baking - **SERVINGS:** 4
INGREDIENTS: Bell peppers, 4 whole; Quinoa, 1 cup; Black beans, 1 cup; Corn, 1 cup; Cherry tomatoes, 1/2 cup; Feta cheese, 1/4 cup; Cilantro, 1/4 cup; Cumin, 1 tsp; Olive oil, 1 Tbsp.; Salt and pepper to taste.

DIRECTIONS: Cook quinoa as instructed; mix with beans, corn, tomatoes, cheese, cilantro, cumin, oil, salt, and pepper. Stuff peppers, bake at 375°F (190°C) until tender.

N.V.: Calories: 250, Fat: 5 g, Carbohydrates: 45 g, Protein: 10 g, Sugar: 5 g, Sodium: 300 mg, Potassium: 670 mg, Cholesterol: 10 mg.

ROSEMARY GARLIC ROASTED CHICKEN

PREP.T.: 15 min **C. T.:** 1 hr 20 min

MODE OF COOKING: Roasting - **SERVINGS:** 6

INGREDIENTS: Chicken, 1 whole (4 lb.); Rosemary, 3 Tbsp.; Garlic, 5 cloves; Olive oil, 2 Tbsp.; Lemon, 1 whole; Salt and pepper to taste.

DIRECTIONS: Rub chicken with olive oil, salt, pepper, minced garlic, and rosemary. Stuff with lemon slices. Roast at 425°F (220°C) until golden and cooked through.

N.V.: Calories: 310, Fat: 13 g, Carbohydrates: 1 g, Protein: 47 g, Sugar: 0 g, Sodium: 95 mg, Potassium: 370 mg, Cholesterol: 125 mg.

SPINACH AND FETA STUFFED MUSHROOMS

PREP.T.: 15 min **C. T.:** 20 min

MODE OF COOKING: Baking - **SERVINGS:** 8

INGREDIENTS: Large mushrooms, 16 whole; Spinach, 2 cups; Feta cheese, 1 cup; Garlic, 2 cloves; Olive oil, 2 Tbsp.; Salt and pepper to taste.

DIRECTIONS: Remove mushroom stems, chop; sauté with garlic, spinach. Mix in feta, stuff mushrooms, drizzle with oil, bake at 350°F (177°C) until tender.

N.V.: Calories: 80, Fat: 5 g, Carbohydrates: 4 g, Protein: 5 g, Sugar: 2 g, Sodium: 200 mg, Potassium: 300 mg, Cholesterol: 15 mg.

CITRUS POMEGRANATE SALAD

PREP.T.: 10 min **C. T.:** 0 min

MODE OF COOKING: Mixing - **SERVINGS:** 4

INGREDIENTS: Mixed greens, 4 cups; Orange, 1 whole; Pomegranate seeds, 1/2 cup; Walnuts, 1/4 cup; Goat cheese, 1/4 cup; Olive oil, 2 Tbsp.; Balsamic vinegar, 1 Tbsp.; Honey, 1 tsp; Salt and pepper to taste.

DIRECTIONS: Peel, segment orange. Toss greens, orange, pomegranate, walnuts, cheese with oil, vinegar, honey, salt, and pepper.

N.V.: Calories: 210, Fat: 15 g, Carbohydrates: 18 g, Protein: 6 g, Sugar: 12 g, Sodium: 125 mg, Potassium: 400 mg, Cholesterol: 10 mg.

BALSAMIC GLAZED BRUSSEL SPROUTS

PREP.T.: 10 min **C. T.:** 25 min

MODE OF COOKING: Roasting - **SERVINGS:** 4

INGREDIENTS: Brussel sprouts, 1 lb.; Balsamic vinegar, 2 Tbsp.; Olive oil, 1 Tbsp.; Honey, 1 tsp; Salt and pepper to taste.

DIRECTIONS: Toss sprouts with oil, salt, pepper; roast at 400°F (204°C) until caramelized. Drizzle with vinegar, honey, roast 5 more min.

N.V.: Calories: 120, Fat: 5 g, Carbohydrates: 17 g, Protein: 4 g, Sugar: 7 g, Sodium: 30 mg, Potassium: 440 mg, Cholesterol: 0 mg.

HERB-INFUSED PRIME RIB

PREP.T.: 20 min **C. T.:** 2 hr

MODE OF COOKING: Roasting - **SERVINGS:** 8

INGREDIENTS: Prime rib roast, 5 lb.; Rosemary, 2 Tbsp.; Thyme, 2 Tbsp.; Garlic, 6 cloves; Olive oil, 3 Tbsp.; Salt and pepper to taste.

DIRECTIONS: Rub roast with oil, garlic, rosemary, thyme, salt, pepper. Roast at 350°F (177°C) until desired doneness. Rest before slicing.

N.V.: Calories: 550, Fat: 42 g, Carbohydrates: 0 g, Protein: 48 g, Sugar: 0 g, Sodium: 110 mg, Potassium: 600 mg, Cholesterol: 135 mg.

SMOKED SALMON CROSTINI

PREP.T.: 15 min **C. T.:** 0 min

MODE OF COOKING: Assembly - **SERVINGS:** 8

INGREDIENTS: Baguette, 1 small; Smoked salmon, 8 oz.; Cream cheese, 4 oz.; Dill, 1/4 cup; Capers, 2 Tbsp.; Lemon, 1 zest; Olive oil, for drizzle; Salt and pepper to taste.

DIRECTIONS: Slice baguette, toast lightly. Spread cream cheese, top with salmon, dill, capers, zest. Drizzle with oil, season with salt, pepper.

N.V.: Calories: 200, Fat: 9 g, Carbohydrates: 18 g, Protein: 12 g, Sugar: 1 g, Sodium: 560 mg, Potassium: 120 mg, Cholesterol: 20 mg.

CHOCOLATE AVOCADO MOUSSE

PREP.T.: 15 min **C. T.:** 0 min

MODE OF COOKING: Blending - **SERVINGS:** 4

INGREDIENTS: Avocado, 2 whole; Cocoa powder, 1/4 cup; Honey, 1/4 cup; Vanilla extract, 1 tsp; Salt, a pinch;

DIRECTIONS: Blend all ingredients until smooth. Chill before serving. Top with fresh berries if desired.

N.V.: Calories: 230, Fat: 15 g, Carbohydrates: 27 g, Protein: 3 g, Sugar: 19 g, Sodium: 10 mg, Potassium: 560 mg, Cholesterol: 0 mg.

PEAR AND GORGONZOLA TART

PREP.T.: 15 min **C. T.:** 25 min

MODE OF COOKING: Baking - **SERVINGS:** 6

INGREDIENTS: Puff pastry, 1 sheet; Pears, 2 large; Gorgonzola cheese, 1/2 cup; Walnuts, 1/4 cup; Honey, 2 Tbsp.; Arugula, 1 cup; Olive oil, 1 Tbsp.; Salt and pepper to taste.

DIRECTIONS: Lay pastry on baking sheet, top with thinly sliced pears, crumble cheese, walnuts; bake at 375°F (190°C) until golden. Top with arugula, drizzle with honey, oil.

N.V.: Calories: 320, Fat: 20 g, Carbohydrates: 30 g, Protein: 6 g, Sugar: 12 g, Sodium: 320 mg, Potassium: 150 mg, Cholesterol: 15 mg.

GRILLED PEACH AND BURRATA SALAD

PREP.T.: 10 min **C. T.:** 5 min

MODE OF COOKING: Grilling - **SERVINGS:** 4

INGREDIENTS: Peaches, 4 halves; Burrata, 8 oz.; Balsamic glaze, 2 Tbsp.; Olive oil, 1 Tbsp.; Basil leaves, 1/4 cup; Salt and pepper to taste.

DIRECTIONS: Grill peaches until charred. Arrange with burrata on plates, drizzle with oil, balsamic glaze. Garnish with basil, season with salt, pepper.

N.V.: Calories: 310, Fat: 22 g, Carbohydrates: 20 g, Protein: 12 g, Sugar: 16 g, Sodium: 400 mg, Potassium: 300 mg, Cholesterol: 60 mg.

LEMON HERB RISOTTO

PREP.T.: 5 min **C. T.:** 25 min

MODE OF COOKING: Stirring - **SERVINGS:** 4

INGREDIENTS: Arborio rice, 1 cup; Chicken broth, 4 cups; Lemon, 1 zest and juice; Parmesan cheese, 1/2 cup; Butter, 2 Tbsp.; Garlic, 1 clove; White wine, 1/2 cup; Parsley, 1/4 cup; Salt and pepper to taste.

DIRECTIONS: Sauté garlic in butter, add rice, toast. Deglaze with wine, add broth gradually, stirring. Finish with lemon, cheese, parsley.

N.V.: Calories: 350, Fat: 10 g, Carbohydrates: 52 g, Protein: 8 g, Sugar: 2 g, Sodium: 900 mg, Potassium: 99 mg, Cholesterol: 25 mg.

PROSCIUTTO WRAPPED ASPARAGUS

PREP.T.: 10 min **C. T.:** 15 min

MODE OF COOKING: Roasting - **SERVINGS:** 4

INGREDIENTS: Asparagus, 1 lb.; Prosciutto, 8 slices; Olive oil, 1 Tbsp.; Parmesan cheese, 2 Tbsp.; Salt and pepper to taste.

DIRECTIONS: Wrap asparagus with prosciutto, drizzle with oil, sprinkle cheese, season. Roast at 400°F (204°C) until tender.

N.V.: Calories: 180, Fat: 12 g, Carbohydrates: 4 g, Protein: 15 g, Sugar: 2 g, Sodium: 570 mg, Potassium: 230 mg, Cholesterol: 30 mg.

CAPRESE SKEWERS WITH BALSAMIC GLAZE

PREP.T.: 10 min **C. T.:** 0 min

MODE OF COOKING: Assembly - **SERVINGS:** 8

INGREDIENTS: Cherry tomatoes, 16; Mozzarella balls, 16; Fresh basil leaves, 32; Balsamic glaze, 2 Tbsp.; Olive oil, 1 Tbsp.; Salt and pepper to taste.

DIRECTIONS: Thread tomato, basil, mozzarella on skewers. Drizzle with oil, balsamic glaze. Season with salt, pepper.

N.V.: Calories: 100, Fat: 7 g, Carbohydrates: 3 g, Protein: 6 g, Sugar: 2 g, Sodium: 200 mg, Potassium: 50 mg, Cholesterol: 20 mg.

SAVORY SPINACH AND ARTICHOKE DIP

PREP.T.: 10 min **C. T.:** 20 min

MODE OF COOKING: Baking - **SERVINGS:** 8

INGREDIENTS: Spinach, 2 cups; Artichoke hearts, 1 cup; Cream cheese, 8 oz.; Sour cream, 1/2 cup; Parmesan cheese, 1/2 cup; Garlic, 2 cloves; Salt and pepper to taste.

DIRECTIONS: Mix all ingredients, bake in a dish at 375°F (190°C) until bubbly. Serve with toasted baguette slices or chips.

N.V.: Calories: 220, Fat: 18 g, Carbohydrates: 7 g, Protein: 8 g, Sugar: 2 g, Sodium: 320 mg, Potassium: 99 mg, Cholesterol: 40 mg.

CONCLUSION

As we come to the close of our journey together through the pages of the "Galveston Diet Cookbook for Beginners," I hope you feel a sense of accomplishment and excitement. Embarking on a path toward better health and wellness is a profound act of self-care, one that requires courage, commitment, and curiosity. You've explored the principles of anti-inflammatory eating, discovered the importance of hormone balance, and unlocked a treasure trove of recipes designed to nourish your body and delight your senses.

The essence of the Galveston Diet is not just about what we eat but how we live. It's a holistic approach that intertwines nutrition with lifestyle, aiming to ignite a transformation that extends beyond the kitchen. This cookbook has aimed to be your companion, guiding you through each meal with simplicity and joy, and providing the tools needed to make healthful eating a sustainable part of your life.

Remember, the journey to wellness is personal and ever-evolving. There will be days of triumph and moments of challenge. The key is to embrace flexibility and forgiveness, allowing yourself to navigate this journey with grace. Health is not a destination but a continuous journey, one that is enriched by each choice we make.

Here are a few takeaways I hope you carry with you:

- **Joy in Simplicity:** The most nourishing meals often come from simple ingredients and preparation methods. Rejoice in the beauty of fresh, whole foods and the magic that happens when they come together on your plate.

- **Mindfulness in Eating:** Listen to your body and its cues. Eating slowly and mindfully enhances the enjoyment of your meals and allows you to tune into the signals of hunger and satiety, fostering a harmonious relationship with food.

- **Flexibility and Balance:** While the foundation of the Galveston Diet is built on anti-inflammatory principles, flexibility is crucial. Allow yourself the grace to enjoy special moments and treats, knowing that one meal does not define your journey.

- **Community and Support:** Sharing meals and experiences with loved ones can amplify your journey to wellness. Don't hesitate to involve your friends and family, creating new traditions around healthful eating and mutual support.

- **Continuous Learning:** The field of nutrition is always evolving. Stay curious, seek out reputable sources of information, and be open to adjusting your approach as you learn more about what works best for your body.

As you continue on your path, remember that every meal is an opportunity to nourish not just your body, but your soul. The Galveston Diet is more than a diet; it's a way of life that celebrates food as a source of healing, joy, and connection. I am honored to have shared this journey with you, and I encourage you to carry forward the principles and practices you've learned, making them a cornerstone of your quest for health and happiness.

Thank you for allowing me to be a part of your journey. May your path be filled with vibrant health, profound wellness, and countless joyous meals shared with those you love. Here's to a life well-nourished, well-lived, and overflowing with vitality.

MEASUREMENT CONVERSION GUIDE

Embarking on a culinary journey with the Galveston Diet can transform your kitchen into a vibrant center of health and wellness. As you navigate through recipes and ingredients, mastering the art of measurement conversions becomes an invaluable skill. This guide is not just a tool; it's your companion in making cooking seamless and stress-free, ensuring that every dish brings you closer to your health goals.

Understanding measurement conversions is akin to learning a new language in the culinary world. It's about fluency in translating teaspoons to milliliters or pounds to grams, making each recipe accessible regardless of the measurement system you're accustomed to. This fluency empowers you to cook with confidence, precision, and a dash of creativity.

When you begin, it's essential to have a set of measuring spoons and cups, ideally both in metric and imperial units. This small investment significantly simplifies the process, allowing you to measure ingredients accurately. But, even with the best tools at hand, there will be moments when conversions are necessary. Perhaps you're trying a recipe that calls for grams, but your scale is lost in the drawer, or you're eyeballing a recipe and need to switch between teaspoons and milliliters. That's where this guide shines.

Let's start with the basics: volume and weight. These are the pillars of culinary measurements, each serving its purpose. Volume is perfect for liquids and some solids like flour, while weight gives you precision, especially for ingredients that can vary significantly in size, like vegetables or meats.

Volume Conversions:
- 1 tablespoon (tbsp) = 3 teaspoons (tsp) = 15 milliliters (ml)
- 1 cup = 16 tablespoons (tbsp) = 8 ounces (oz) = 240 milliliters (ml)
- 1 pint (pt) = 2 cups = 16 ounces (oz) = 480 milliliters (ml)
- 1 quart (qt) = 2 pints (pt) = 4 cups = 32 ounces (oz) = 960 milliliters (ml)
- 1 gallon (gal) = 4 quarts (qt) = 8 pints (pt) = 16 cups = 128 ounces (oz) = 3.785 liters (l)

Weight Conversions:
- 1 ounce (oz) = 28.35 grams (g)
- 1 pound (lb) = 16 ounces (oz) = 453.59 grams (g)

Temperature conversions are equally important, especially when baking. The precision in baking temperature can make or break a recipe. For those moments when you're faced with a recipe in Fahrenheit and your oven is calibrated in Celsius, remember:

- To convert Fahrenheit to Celsius, subtract 32 from the Fahrenheit value and multiply by 5/9.
- To convert Celsius to Fahrenheit, multiply the Celsius value by 9/5 and add 32.

Lastly, a tip that goes beyond numbers: trust your instincts. Measurements can guide you, but your senses are irreplaceable tools. The aroma of a simmering stew, the texture of dough beneath your fingers, and the golden hue of a perfectly baked cake are all signs that you're on the right path.

This guide is your starting point, a foundation upon which you can build your culinary adventures. With practice, converting measurements will become second nature, allowing you to focus on the joy of cooking and the satisfaction of nourishing your body with delicious, anti-inflammatory meals. Remember, every teaspoon and tablespoon, every gram and ounce, brings you closer to mastering the art of healthy cooking.

SCAN QR CODE TO DOWNLOAD EXTRA CONTENT

Volume Equivalents (Liquid)

US Standard	US Standard (ounces)	Metric (approximate)
2 tablespoons	1 fl. oz.	30 mL
¼ cup	2 fl. oz.	60 mL
half cup	4 fl. oz.	120 mL
1 cup	8 fl. oz.	240 mL
1 half cups	12 fl. oz.	355 mL
2 cups or 1 pint	16 fl. oz.	457 mL
4 cups or 1 quart	32 fl. oz.	1 L
1 gallon	128 fl. oz.	4 L

Volume Equivalents (Dry)

US Standard	Metric (approximate)
1/8 teaspoon	0.5 mL
¼ teaspoon	1 mL
half teaspoon	2 mL
¾ teaspoon	4 mL
1 teaspoon	5 mL
1 tablespoon	15 mL
¼ cup	59 mL
1/3 cup	79 mL
half cup	118 mL
2/3 cup	156 mL
¾ cup	177 mL

1 cup	235 mL
2 cups or 1 pint	475 mL
3 cups	700 mL
4 cups or 1 quart	1 L

Oven Temperatures

Fahrenheit (F)	Celsius (C) (approximate)
250°F	120°C
300°F	150°C
325°F	165°C
350°F	180°C
375°F	190°C
400°F	200°C
425°F	220°C
450°F	230°C

Weight Equivalents

US Standard	Metric (approximate)
1 tablespoon	15 g
half ounce	15 g
1 ounce	30 g
2 ounces	60 g
4 ounces	115 g
8 ounces	225 g
12 ounces	340 g
16 ounces or 1 pound or 1 lb	455 g

28-DAY MEAL PLAN

I'm thrilled to share with you the latest chapter in your wellness journey: the Meal Plan, meticulously designed to align with the Galveston Diet principles. This plan is crafted to further enhance your experience with a diverse array of flavors, nutrients, and, most importantly, health benefits rooted in anti-inflammatory eating. We've ventured beyond the ordinary to ensure each meal is a step towards optimal wellness, balancing your hormones, and igniting your metabolism, all while delighting your taste buds.

In this plan, you'll find a fresh selection of recipes that have been carefully chosen to avoid repetition, ensuring each day brings something new and exciting to your table. From the energizing breakfasts to kick-start your mornings to the nourishing dinners that wind down your day, we've covered every meal and snack in between with your health and enjoyment in mind.

DAY	BREAKFAST	SNACK 1	LUNCH	SNACK 2	DINNER
1	BLUEBERRY WALNUT SMOOTHIE BOWL	CHIA SEED PUDDING WITH MIXED BERRIES	SWEET POTATO AND BLACK BEAN BREAKFAST BURRITO	GREEN GODDESS SMOOTHIE	QUINOA BREAKFAST BOWL
2	EGG MUFFINS WITH SPINACH AND FETA	ALMOND BUTTER AND BANANA OPEN SANDWICH	TURMERIC GINGER OATMEAL	AVOCADO TOAST WITH POACHED EGG	GREEN GODDESS SMOOTHIE
3	COTTAGE CHEESE AND PEACH PARFAIT	VEGAN SWEET POTATO AND BLACK BEAN CHILI	GARLIC HERB ROASTED CHICKEN WITH VEGETABLES	PARMESAN ZUCCHINI AND CORN	SPINACH AND QUINOA SALAD WITH LEMON VINAIGRETTE
4	TURKEY AVOCADO WRAP	MEDITERRANEAN LENTIL SALAD	CHICKPEA SALAD SANDWICH	SOBA NOODLE AND EDAMAME BOWL	ROASTED VEGETABLE AND HUMMUS PITA
5	SMOKED SALMON AND CREAM CHEESE BAGEL	SPICY THAI PEANUT CHICKEN WRAP	GRILLED VEGETABLE QUINOA SALAD	CAULIFLOWER BUFFALO WRAPS	POMEGRANATE CHICKEN SALAD
6	AVOCADO QUINOA STUFFED TOMATOES	TUNA AND BEAN SALAD	EGGPLANT CAPRESE SANDWICH	SPICY TURKEY LETTUCE WRAPS	BEETROOT AND GOAT CHEESE SALAD
7	CURRIED CHICKEN SALAD WITH GRAPES	VEGETARIAN SUSHI BOWL	MANGO CHICKEN SALAD WITH LIME DRESSING	SALMON WITH CRISPY KALE AND QUINOA	GRILLED CHICKPEA AND VEGETABLE TACOS

DAY	BREAKFAST	SNACK 1	LUNCH	SNACK 2	DINNER
8	BLUEBERRY WALNUT SMOOTHIE BOWL	PEANUT BUTTER ENERGY BALLS	SPINACH AND QUINOA SALAD WITH LEMON VINAIGRETTE	ROASTED BRUSSELS SPROUTS WITH BACON	SALMON WITH CRISPY KALE AND QUINOA
9	CHIA SEED PUDDING WITH MIXED BERRIES	CRISPY CHICKPEA AND TURMERIC SNACK	TURKEY AVOCADO WRAP	SPICY LIME ROASTED NUTS	GRILLED CHICKPEA AND VEGETABLE TACOS
10	SWEET POTATO AND BLACK BEAN BREAKFAST BURRITO	AVOCADO AND COTTAGE CHEESE DIP	MEDITERRANEAN LENTIL SALAD	GARLIC AND HERB MASHED CAULIFLOWER	BEEF AND BROCCOLI STIR-FRY
11	GREEN GODDESS SMOOTHIE	SWEET POTATO CHIPS	CHICKPEA SALAD SANDWICH	BAKED PARMESAN TOMATO SLICES	MEDITERRANEAN STUFFED EGGPLANT
12	QUINOA BREAKFAST BOWL	ZUCCHINI AND PARMESAN FRITTERS	SOBA NOODLE AND EDAMAME BOWL	CINNAMON ROASTED SWEET POTATOES	ROASTED BUTTERNUT SQUASH AND CHICKPEA SALAD
13	EGG MUFFINS WITH SPINACH AND FETA	KALE AND ALMOND PESTO	ROASTED VEGETABLE AND HUMMUS PITA	CHILLED CUCUMBER SOUP	LEMON GARLIC TILAPIA
14	ALMOND BUTTER AND BANANA OPEN SANDWICH	CUCUMBER AND DILL YOGURT SALAD	SMOKED SALMON AND CREAM CHEESE BAGEL	QUINOA TABBOULEH	THAI COCONUT CURRY TOFU

DAY	BREAKFAST	SNACK 1	LUNCH	SNACK 2	DINNER
15	TURMERIC GINGER OATMEAL	HUMMUS AND VEGETABLE PLATTER	POMEGRANATE CHICKEN SALAD	CINNAMON SPICED BAKED PEARS	MANGO CHICKEN SALAD WITH LIME DRESSING
16	AVOCADO TOAST WITH POACHED EGG	CHEESY KALE CHIPS	AVOCADO QUINOA STUFFED TOMATOES	LEMON RICOTTA BERRY PARFAIT	LEMON-HERB GRILLED SALMON
17	VEGAN SWEET POTATO AND BLACK BEAN CHILI	ROASTED RED PEPPER HUMMUS	TUNA AND BEAN SALAD	GINGER PEAR SORBET	SHRIMP AND AVOCADO TACOS
18	GARLIC HERB ROASTED CHICKEN WITH VEGETABLES	BAKED SWEET POTATO FRIES	EGGPLANT CAPRESE SANDWICH	COCONUT DUSTED CHOCOLATE FIGS	BAKED COD WITH CRISPY PARMESAN CRUST
19	PARMESAN ZUCCHINI AND CORN	CREAMY AVOCADO DIP	BEETROOT AND GOAT CHEESE SALAD	ALMOND JOY ENERGY BALLS	GARLIC LEMON SCALLOPS
20	SPICY THAI PEANUT CHICKEN WRAP	SPICY PUMPKIN SEEDS	CURRIED CHICKEN SALAD WITH GRAPES	MAPLE CINNAMON ROASTED ALMONDS	SPICY TUNA STUFFED AVOCADOS
21	CAULIFLOWER BUFFALO WRAPS	BLACKBERRY BALSAMIC BLISS BITES	VEGETARIAN SUSHI BOWL	HONEY-LIME YOGURT FRUIT SALAD	MEDITERRANEAN SEA BASS EN PAPILLOTE

DAY	BREAKFAST	SNACK 1	LUNCH	SNACK 2	DINNER
22	PARMESAN HERB CRUSTED HALIBUT	PISTACHIO-CRUSTED CHOCOLATE DATES	BALSAMIC GLAZED BEEF STEAK	CUCUMBER LEMON DETOX WATER	BEEF STIR-FRY WITH BROCCOLI AND PEPPERS
23	SPICY GRILLED OCTOPUS	VANILLA BEAN AND BERRY POPSICLES	TURKEY MEATBALLS WITH SPINACH	TURMERIC GINGER TEA	CHICKEN PICCATA WITH CAPERS
24	HERB-INFUSED MUSSELS	CACAO NIB AND SEA SALT DARK CHOCOLATE BARK	SPICY BEEF AND BROCCOLI STIR-FRY	BEETROOT AND BERRY SMOOTHIE	SLOW COOKER TURKEY CHILI
25	COCONUT SHRIMP CURRY	ZESTY LEMON SQUARES	HERBED CHICKEN PARMESAN	CARROT GINGER JUICE	BALSAMIC BEEF SHORT RIBS
26	FISH TACOS WITH MANGO SALSA	SPICED ROASTED CHICKPEAS	SLOW-COOKED BEEF RAGU	SPARKLING MINT LIMEADE	GRILLED CHICKEN WITH MANGO SALSA
27	LEMON BUTTER SCALLOPS WITH PARSLEY	MATCHA GREEN TEA TRUFFLES	GRILLED TURKEY BURGERS WITH AVOCADO	WATERMELON COCONUT HYDRATOR	SPINACH AND STRAWBERRY SALAD
28	ROSEMARY GARLIC CHICKEN BREASTS	GREEN TEA LIME MINT REFRESHER	LEMON DILL ROAST CHICKEN	ALMOND MILK CHAI LATTE	QUINOA AND BLACK BEAN SALAD

Made in the USA
Columbia, SC
19 September 2024